125 best Entertaining Recipes

Julia Aitken

Robert ROSE

For complete cataloguing information, see page 185.

Disclaimers
The recipes in this book have been carefully tested by our kitchen and our tasters. To the best of our knowledge, they are safe and nutritious for ordinary use and users. For those people with food or other allergies, or who have special food requirements or health issues, please read the suggested contents of each recipe carefully and determine whether or not they may create a problem for you. All recipes are used at the risk of the consumer.

We cannot be responsible for any hazards, loss or damage that may occur as a result of any recipe use.

For those with special needs, allergies, requirements or health problems, in the event of any doubt, please contact your medical adviser prior to the use of any recipe.

Design and Production: Joseph Gisini/PageWave Graphics Inc.
Indexer: Barbara Schon
Cover Photography: Colin Erricson
Interior Photography: Mark T. Shapiro
Food Styling: Kate Bush
Prop Styling: Charlene Erricson

The publisher and author wish to express their appreciation to the following supplier of props used in the food photography appearing in the book:

Dishes, cutlery, linens and accessories:
HomeFront, 371 Eglinton Avenue W., Toronto, (416) 488-3189, *www. homefrontshop.com*

Cover image: Tandoori Chicken (see recipe, page 20)

We acknowledge the financial support of the Government of Canada through the Book Publishing Industry Development Program (BPIDP) for our publishing activities.

Published by Robert Rose Inc.
120 Eglinton Avenue East, Suite 800, Toronto, Ontario, Canada M4P 1E2
Tel: (416) 322-6552 Fax: (416) 322-6936

Printed in Canada

1 2 3 4 5 6 7 8 9 CPL 15 14 13 12 11 10 09 08 07

Contents

Acknowledgments

Writing a cookbook always requires the dedication and enthusiasm of far more people than simply the writer whose name appears on the cover. Now is their chance to shine. Many thanks to:

Publisher Bob Dees, who would put many an eminent psychologist to shame with his uncanny ability to weed out just what each of his authors' food passions are then persuade them to write a book about it.

My unflappable agent Denise Schon who, on more than one occasion, said, "don't worry; leave everything to me." I did and she never let me down.

Recipe testers Joyce Parslow, Claire Arfin and Jan Main, who did a terrific job fine-tuning my recipes, despite the ridiculous deadlines.

Wine writer David Lawrason, for sharing his encyclopedic knowledge of wine.

Peter Matthews for his editorial expertise.

Joseph Gisini of PageWave Graphics for his wonderful design.

Colin Erricson for his stunning cover photography and Mark Shapiro for his equally fabulous inside shots.

Kate Bush, equally adept at being food stylist and friend, for making my recipes look even better than I thought possible.

Prop stylist Charlene Erricson, for choosing picture-perfect dishes and linens.

My husband, Iain, for his love and support but mainly for his patience.

My friends, all of them special people in my life, but particularly to Liz Paterson, Di Chase, Julie Cohen, Ruth Davies, Tracy John, John Fitzgerald, Gérard Hernando, Bruce Kemp and Maureen Delaney, who are always there for me with advice, meals and/or glasses of wine and, best of all, who make me laugh.

The food writers and chefs I've met over the years who have always been quick to share their knowledge and enthusiasm for the good things in life — especially Rose Murray and Anita Stewart, who both added love and friendship to the mix.

The coffee-growers of Colombia for helping to keep me awake.

For Mary, Patrick and Lucy,
in memory of Mum and Dad
who always entertained with style.

Entertaining 101

Let's get two things straight right off the top: Number one, inviting friends over for dinner doesn't have to be scary or stressful; number two, there are no food police. A certain blond is not going to burst into your kitchen brandishing a glue gun if you screw something up or if you cheat.

Which is fortunate because cheating is a big part of entertaining. There isn't a chef in this world who single-handedly prepares, serves and clears up meals for his customers. There's always a highly trained team of helpers — both in the kitchen and out front — scurrying around helping to make Chef look good. So, why is it, when we entertain at home, we think we must do *everything* ourselves?

Here's where the cheating comes in. If you absolutely love to cook and think there's no better way to spend a day than puttering in the kitchen preparing for a dinner party (and I have to confess, I'm one of those weird people who do), then go ahead and make the whole meal from scratch.

If, on the other hand, you have a life, prepare an appetizer and main course, but buy a beautiful fruit pie for dessert, or simply serve fresh fruit and a selection of cheeses for "afters." If you'd prefer to create a luscious dessert yourself, then opt for a simple pasta main course to serve with purchased bread and a salad of mesclun, those baby greens now available in most large supermarkets.

Which brings us to grocery shopping. Who has the time? So, all the recipes in this book use ingredients available in most large supermarkets with just one or two detours needed to your local bulk-food store for items such as dried fruits.

I've structured this book to reflect a typical menu and you'll find dishes here that can be mixed and matched. There are nibbles to snack on with drinks while dinner's cooking, appetizers and soups to eat at the dining table, followed by main courses, accompaniments, salads then desserts. Feel free to create a whole meal from the book, or simply select an appetizer or a dessert you like the sound of and team it with a favorite main course of your own.

Whatever you choose to do, remember to have fun cooking and don't try to tackle more than you can comfortably handle. Your guests would far rather enjoy a simple meal, in the company of a relaxed and happy host, than plow through a six-course banquet while you collapse frazzled and exhausted in the corner.

My Top Twenty Tips For Entertaining

1. Don't entertain people you don't like. There's no rule that says you *have* to invite someone over for dinner; you'll enjoy yourself and be more relaxed with people you prefer.

2. Lots of planning is the easiest route to a stress-free evening. Think about your guest list and menu well ahead of time, and prepare any of the dishes that can be made in advance. Don't choose a menu that needs a lot of last-minute preparation and don't be afraid to accept help, either in the days leading up to the party or during the event itself.

3. When putting together your menu, a quick glance over the recipes you're planning to prepare should tell you if they're a good match. Three courses packed with cream and/or eggs will probably result in too rich a meal for your guests to fully enjoy. Likewise, don't select dishes with similar flavors: A soup, main course and dessert that all contain cinnamon would be a dull combination. Keep colors in mind, too. Sole fillets with mashed potato cry out for a green vegetable or a simple tomato salad to add a little pizzazz to the plate.

4. If you're inviting people you've never fed before, call them in advance of planning your menu to check if they have any food allergies or other dietary restrictions.

5. Unless you're catering a backyard barbecue for 50, don't serve the food on paper or plastic plates. Not only does the food not taste as good, it sends an odd message to your guests: I don't care enough about you to bother washing up afterwards. The same goes for plastic glasses.

6. Tempting though it may be to save on laundry, avoid using paper napkins — unless it's to hand round with any snacks before dinner. At the table, cloth napkins make all the difference.

7. Candles placed strategically around a room always add atmosphere, but avoid using scented ones, which can over-power the taste of the food.

8. Having the table laid well ahead of your guests' arrival not only gets one task out of the way but also shows you're expecting them and makes your guests feel welcome.

9. Although it's not always necessary to arrange your guests around the table in a boy-girl-boy-girl configuration, take a little time to think about a seating plan that doesn't put all the shy people at one end of the table. Remember, good conversation contributes as much to the success of the evening as the food and wine.

10. Don't lose sleep because you feel incapable of creating a fancy centerpiece for your table. Fresh flowers plunked in a short vase (so your guests can see each other across the table) will do fine.

11. Serving one or two of the easy pre-dinner nibbles (see pages 13 to 24) when your guests arrive helps to pace the evening, allows time for any late-comers to show up and gives your guests something to do while you're putting the finishing touches to the appetizer or main course.

12. It may seem obvious, but always serve hot food on hot plates, cold food on cold plates.

13. Even if you expect your guests to turn up toting a bottle, don't rely on them to provide all the wine. They might show up with their Uncle Bob's homemade Chianti which, of course, you will accept gratefully but not open until you've absolutely run out of everything else. For more information on selecting wine for a meal, see A Word About Wine (page 12).

14. Recruit someone you can rely on — your life partner or a close friend — to take charge of refilling your guests' glasses; that way, you can concentrate on the food. There's nothing worse than having a guest nursing an empty glass for an hour because the host is too busy scampering round the kitchen.

15. For simplicity's sake, I usually confine the choice of alcoholic beverages to red or white wine or beer. Reckon on needing about half a bottle of wine per person, and always have an interesting selection of non-alcoholic drinks — such as flavored and unflavored mineral waters, fruit juices or pop — on hand for drivers and other guests who don't drink alcohol.

16. A large jug of iced water (filtered or mineral water) on the table with slices of lemon, orange or lime floating in it looks pretty and offers your guests an alternative to wine if they prefer it.

17. If you're cooking several dishes, prepare any garnishes ahead of time and keep a checklist of these last-minute additions. I can't tell you the number of times I've opened the fridge at the end of an evening to find little bowls of chopped this and that which failed to make it to their appointed place on top of the casserole or dessert.

18. Post a simple timetable on the fridge to remind you, say, to remove the dessert from the fridge as you and your guests sit down to the main course.

19. When I entertain, I try to have everything done about half an hour before everyone arrives, which gives me just enough time to run through the shower, slap on some make-up, then sit quietly for five minutes and enjoy a glass of wine. That way, at least I *look* relaxed when my guests arrive.

20. Finally, always remember that your primary task as host is to make your guests feel welcome, comfortable and relaxed. Your friends are coming not as food critics, but to spend time with you. If you keep things simple, you'll be pleasant company too.

The Prudent Host's Pantry

Successful, stress-free entertaining depends on good, simple food, but that also means using the best-quality ingredients you can find. Here are just a few of the basics which will make all the difference to your cooking.

Black pepper — Always buy whole peppercorns and grind them in a pepper mill.

Butter — There is no substitute for butter in cakes and desserts. It has the best flavor so, please, don't be tempted to use margarine.

Chocolate — For most recipes it's best to buy good-quality eating (not baking) chocolate. If the label specifies the percentage of cocoa solids in the chocolate, so much the better: Look for chocolate with about 70% cocoa solids.

Dried mushrooms — These are well worth having in your pantry and you'll notice they appear in several recipes in this book. Just a few dried mushrooms, such as porcini (available in the produce section of most large supermarkets), add a wonderful earthy flavor to all kinds of dishes, from pasta sauces to pot roasts.

Garlic — There is no substitute for fresh garlic. And since it keeps well at room temperature, there's really no excuse for buying ready-minced garlic or that dreadful garlic powder.

Ginger — For best flavor, use fresh ginger and mince it yourself. In an emergency, however — and here ginger is unlike garlic which should always be used fresh — small jars of minced ginger (available in the produce section of most large supermarkets) are quite a good alternative to fresh ginger.

Herbs — As a rule, fresh herbs have the best flavor. In many recipes, however, dried herbs are a perfectly good alternative. (Use about half to one-third the amount of dried herbs as you would fresh.) The only exceptions here are fresh parsley and chives, for which there are no good dried substitutes. Also, of course, dried herbs don't make a terribly attractive garnish.

Ice cream — Buy the best-quality ice cream you can find, especially for my super-simple Cheat's Desserts (see pages 180-184).

Lemon/Lime/ Orange juice — Always squeeze fresh lemons or limes for juice; the ready-squeezed juice is too acidic and just doesn't have the same flavor. However, in a pinch, you can use good-quality (not from concentrate) orange juice out of a carton as a substitute for fresh orange juice.

Liquor — Unless you have an extensive bar at home, buy miniature bottles of liquor needed for cooking; each contains $\frac{1}{4}$ cup (50 mL).

Maple syrup — Always buy the real thing rather than "maple-flavored" syrup; you'll find you need far less to add distinctive maple flavor to your food.

Nutmeg	For best flavor, always grate your own nutmeg. Whole nutmegs will last for years when stored in a sealed jar in a dark cupboard, but ready-grated nutmeg goes stale very quickly.
Nuts	Nuts go rancid very quickly, so buy them in small sealed packages and store them in the freezer. The soapy taste of rancid nuts will ruin any dish to which they're added.
Oil	I generally use olive oil or canola oil for cooking. To ensure the best-flavored olive oil, look for the words "cold-pressed" and "extra virgin" on the label.
Olives	Always buy good-quality olives from the deli section of your supermarket. Although there are some quite decent olives available in jars, never buy canned olives; their flavor just isn't as good.
Parmesan cheese	There are few guarantees in life but I can promise you one thing: Once you've tasted real Parmesan cheese (it will have the words "Parmigiano-Reggiano" stamped on its rind) you will never go back to the containers of ready-grated stuff. Genuine Parmesan is expensive but it has such a full, rich flavor that a little goes a long way; it will keep for weeks in the refrigerator if you wrap it in wax paper then pop it in a sealable plastic bag.
Pasta	Good-quality pasta has a much better texture, will keep its shape after cooking and is not so easy to overcook as cheaper brands.
Rice	Don't buy any type of instant rice: it has an unpleasant mushy texture.
Stock	The best stock is good robust homemade stock (see Giblet Stock, page 84), but a good alternative is canned low-sodium chicken or beef broth.
Tomatoes	Never, ever refrigerate tomatoes; their texture goes strangely woolly. The best tomatoes are local ones bought in season. At other times of the year, however, you can find some quite acceptable hothouse tomatoes, usually sold with their stems intact.
Vanilla	Always use pure vanilla extract. It's a little more expensive than the artificial alternatives, but the flavor is much better and you'll find you won't need to use as much.
Whipping cream	Yes, I know it's sinful. But just a little makes *such* a difference to a dish. Like butter, there really is no substitute.
Wine	Bad wine tastes bad, whatever you do with it. And while I wouldn't suggest using a $500 bottle of vintage Bordeaux for cooking, you should only cook with a wine you'd be prepared to drink. A good rule of thumb is to cook with the same wine you're planning to serve with the dish.

Dinner Party Survival Kit

With the following items in my freezer, fridge or pantry, I find I can quickly put together simple appetizers and desserts, leaving me more time to concentrate on the main course.

Freezer

Ready-sliced smoked salmon: Serve it as an appetizer with thinly sliced, lightly buttered whole wheat bread and lemon wedges on the side.

Italian-style bread: Buy the kind you need to bake for a few minutes before serving. It's a perfect accompaniment to most soups and many main dishes, from pastas to casseroles.

Italian-style flatbread: Use for a quick pizza (page 62) or add one of the focaccia toppings on page 53.

Pita breads: Use to make a quick homemade alternative to chips (page 18).

Good-quality blanched almonds: Toss them in hot olive oil in a small skillet; drain on paper towels, sprinkle with salt and serve warm.

Puff pastry: This keeps for months in the freezer and takes very little time to thaw. Use to make a simple appetizer, such as Tomato and Blue Cheese Tart (page 29), or prepare cheese sticks for a pre-dinner nibble: Roll out pastry thinly, sprinkle generously with freshly grated Parmesan cheese; cut into thin strips and transfer to a baking sheet, twisting strips as you do so. Bake in a 400°F (200°C) oven for 8 to 10 minutes, until golden brown and crisp. Serve warm or cold.

Good-quality vanilla ice cream: Team it with one of the sauces in the Cheat's Desserts section (pages 180 to 184) and/or fresh fruit for the fastest dessert possible.

A selection of frozen fruit (berries, peaches, rhubarb): Thawed berries or peaches can be blended until smooth then sweetened to taste and served as a fresh-tasting sauce to drizzle over ice cream or pound cake. Rhubarb can be used in all kinds of desserts, from pies to cobblers.

Refrigerator

A selection of olives from the deli section of your supermarket: Heap in a bowl alongside cubed feta and cherry tomatoes for an instant pre-dinner nibble.

A selection of domestic and imported cheeses: Serve with olives, pickles and crackers for a speedy appetizer, or team with fresh fruit — grapes, apples and pears — and a good-quality nut bread for an equally quick dessert. In either case, remember to let the cheese stand (still in its wrapper) at room temperature for 30 minutes to 1 hour before serving.

Pesto: This is a vibrant-flavored Italian condiment made from basil, olive oil and garlic; look for it where sauces and condiments are sold in your supermarket. Spread it thinly on slices of lightly toasted Italian bread, then top with chopped or sliced tomatoes for a quick bruschetta.

Pantry

Olive oil and balsamic vinegar: Whisk these together in a ratio of three parts oil to one part vinegar, then add salt and pepper to taste for a flavorful dressing to toss with all kinds of salad greens. Alternatively, the same ratio of oil and vinegar poured into a shallow dish (do not whisk, and omit salt and pepper) makes a great dip for warm Italian bread.

Brandy: A splash of brandy and a sprinkling of sugar is a quick way to perk up a bowl of fresh berries.

A Word About Wine

There are many writers far better qualified than I to discuss matching wines with food. And if you want to get into pairing food and wine in a serious way, there are many excellent books on the subject that should be available in the wine section of your local bookstore. I can, however, offer a few hints and tips that I've found helpful over the years.

If you're planning a themed meal and are serving foods of a specific country, choose the wine of that country to drink with it: Italian wine with an Italian menu, Spanish wine with a Spanish menu, Indian beer with an Indian meal (although fruity whites, such as gerwurztraminer, also go well with spicy Indian food).

Light foods are best teamed with light wine, heavier dishes with full-bodied wine. How to tell the style of a wine? As a general rule, higher-alcohol wines — those from warm wine-producing regions, like Spain, Greece, Italy, southern France, California and Australia — tend to be fuller-bodied; lower-alcohol wines from cooler climates — such as mid- and western France, New Zealand, the Pacific northwest and Germany — tend to be lighter.

David Lawrason, a wine educator and editor of *Wine Access* magazine, has devised the following general guidelines for matching food and wine. Following the wine styles are the grape varieties (in parentheses) to look for on the wine label.

With...	Serve a...
oysters or mussels	light, dry white (muscadet or sauvignon blanc)
lobster or shrimp	medium- to full-bodied dry white (chardonnay)
fish with lemon or white sauce	medium-bodied dry white (sauvignon, chardonnay) or a fruity white (riesling or chenin)
smoked fish	rosé or blush (grenache), a light red (gamay) or a full-bodied white (chardonnay)
poultry	full-bodied white (chardonnay or sauvignon) or a light- to medium-bodied red (pinot noir or zinfandel)
light meat, such as pork	full-bodied white (chardonnay), a semi-sweet white (riesling or chenin) or a light red (gamay)
red meat, such as beef or lamb	medium- to full-bodied red (cabernet sauvignon, pinot noir, syrah or merlot)
light pasta dishes	dry white (chardonnay or any Italian white wine)
tomato-based pasta dishes	medium-bodied red (zinfandel or any Italian red)
vegetarian dishes	dry white (sauvignon blanc)
mild cheese	full-bodied white (sauvignon blanc) or a medium-bodied red (pinot noir)
strong cheese	full-bodied red (cabernet sauvignon) or a fortified wine, such as port
fruit-based desserts	dessert wine (riesling or semillon)
chocolate desserts	fortified wine, such as port or sweet sherry

Pre-dinner Nibbles

Thai-roasted shrimp

Makes about 35 shrimp

These moist, flavorful shrimp can be served hot or cold. Do not marinate longer than 1 hour or the shrimp will become mushy.

Kitchen Wisdom

A folded damp cloth placed under your chopping board will keep it in place while you chop.

Sesame oil is a vibrantly flavored oil that frequently appears in Asian recipes. It has a strong flavor, so use sparingly. Look for sesame oil in the Asian section of your supermarket. It will be labeled as pure sesame oil or as a blend of sesame and soybean oils — either type is fine for this recipe.

- Large shallow nonreactive dish
- Baking sheet, lightly oiled

1 lb	raw large shrimp, in their shells	500 g
	Grated zest of 2 limes	
	Freshly squeezed juice of 2 limes	
2 tbsp	sesame oil	25 mL
2 tbsp	chopped fresh coriander	25 mL
1	clove garlic, minced	1
$1/2$ tsp	hot pepper sauce	2 mL
$1/4$ tsp	salt	1 mL
	Lettuce leaves	

1. Remove shells from shrimp, leaving tails and last segment of shell intact. If necessary, with a small sharp knife, slit backs of shrimp just enough to remove dark vein-like intestinal tract from each. Pat shrimp dry on paper towels.

2. In the nonreactive dish, combine lime zest, lime juice, sesame oil, coriander, garlic, hot pepper sauce and salt. Add shrimp; stir gently. Refrigerate, covered, for 1 hour.

3. Preheat the oven to 400°F (200°C). Remove shrimp from marinade, shaking off any excess. Arrange in a single layer on baking sheet. Bake for 5 to 7 minutes or until shrimp are just pink. Do not overcook. Serve hot or cold on a lettuce-lined platter.

> ### Make Ahead
> If serving shrimp cold, cook then refrigerate, covered, for up to 24 hours.

Date and cheese bites

Makes 24

These are among my favorite finger foods. They're embarrassingly easy to make and guests rave about them. The sharp, salty tang of Romano cheese goes beautifully with the sweet rich flavor of the dates. If you can't find Romano cheese, extra-old Cheddar cheese is a good substitute.

These stuffed dates are good served with the Watermelon and Cherry-Tomato Brochettes (see recipe, page 16).

Kitchen Wisdom

Use fancy pitted dates instead of cooking dates.

| 24 | dates | 24 |
| 3 oz | Romano cheese, cut into 24 small pieces | 75 g |

1. If dates are unpitted, cut a slit in one side of each date without cutting in half; remove pit. If dates are already pitted, slightly enlarge the existing slit in each.

2. Tuck 1 piece of cheese into each date. Serve at room temperature.

> **Make Ahead**
> Stuffed dates can be refrigerated, covered, for up to 24 hours.

Watermelon and cherry-tomato brochettes

Makes 30

The wonderful combination of flavors in these brochettes provide an excellent example of how great food needn't be complicated. I first enjoyed them at El Bulli, a three-Michelin-starred restaurant north of Barcelona in Spain, where chef-owner Ferran Adriá prepared an extraordinary 25-course lunch for our group of visiting food writers and chefs. As you'd expect, some of the dishes were incredibly complex but others, like these brochettes, were surprisingly simple.

Buy small cherry tomatoes (they should be about the same size as the watermelon balls) or cut larger cherry tomatoes in half.

Encourage your guests to eat the brochettes in one bite to fully appreciate the mix of flavors.

Kitchen Wisdom

A melon baller is an inexpensive investment that's useful for other chores, such as removing cores from pears.

• 30 toothpicks

30	watermelon balls (from 1 large slice)	30
30	fresh basil leaves	30
30	small cherry tomatoes	30

1. Thread 1 watermelon ball, 1 basil leaf then 1 cherry tomato on each toothpick. Arrange on a platter; serve at room temperature.

> **Make Ahead**
> The brochettes can be refrigerated, tightly covered with plastic wrap, for up to 4 hours. Let stand at room temperature for 30 minutes before serving.

Madrid mushrooms

Makes 25

In their native Spain, these morsels would be stuffed with satiny-smooth air-dried Ibérico or Serrano ham. Sadly, it's difficult to find either ham in North America, so I've substituted Italian prosciutto, which is almost as good.

Kitchen Wisdom

If using very lean prosciutto, you'll need only 2 oz (50 g).

If you don't have a garlic press, use a knife to mince the garlic very finely.

Reserve mushroom stems for use in another recipe, such as soup or stock.

• Baking sheet

25	button mushrooms (about 1$^1/_2$ inches/4 cm in diameter), wiped with damp paper towels, stems discarded	25
1 tbsp	olive oil	15 mL
$^1/_4$ tsp	black pepper	1 mL
Pinch	salt	Pinch
3 oz	prosciutto, trimmed of excess fat and finely chopped	75 g
$^1/_4$ cup	mayonnaise	50 mL
1	small clove garlic, pressed through a garlic press	1
	Watercress (tough stems discarded)	
	Paprika	

1. Preheat oven to 400°F (200°C). In a medium bowl, combine mushrooms, olive oil, pepper and salt; toss well.

2. Arrange mushrooms, stem-side up, in a single layer on baking sheet. Divide prosciutto evenly among mushroom caps. Bake for 10 to 15 minutes or until tender and juicy.

3. Meanwhile, in a small bowl, combine mayonnaise and garlic; stir until well combined.

4. When mushrooms are ready, spoon a small dollop of mayonnaise on top of each. Arrange mushrooms on a serving platter; surround with watercress. Sprinkle mushrooms very lightly with paprika. Serve at once.

> **Make Ahead**
> Stuffed mushrooms can be refrigerated, covered, for up to 4 hours before baking. Garlic mayonnaise can be refrigerated, covered, for up to 24 hours.

Pâté with pita crisps and onion marmalade

Serves 8 to 10

There are so many good-quality pâtés available in supermarkets these days that it hardly seems worth making your own — but it's good to find a new way of serving it. Here, the pâté is spread on crisp pita wedges and served with a sweet-tart onion chutney.

Be sure to buy the type of pita breads that have a "pocket" in them; otherwise you won't be able to split them horizontally.

• Baking sheet

2 tbsp	canola oil or vegetable oil	25 mL
2	medium red onions, halved and thinly sliced	2
¾ tsp	salt	4 mL
¾ tsp	black pepper	4 mL
¼ tsp	ground cloves	1 mL
2 tbsp	granulated sugar	25 mL
2 tbsp	balsamic vinegar	25 mL
4	7-inch (17.5 cm) pita breads	4
	Olive-oil baking spray	
1	package (7 oz/200 g) pâté	1
	Boston lettuce leaves	

1. In a large heavy saucepan, heat oil over medium-high heat. Add onions, ¼ tsp (1 mL) salt, ¼ tsp (1 mL) pepper and cloves; stir thoroughly. Reduce heat to low; cook, covered, for 15 minutes. Add sugar and vinegar. Cook, covered and stirring occasionally, for 30 to 40 minutes or until onions are very tender. Add more sugar or vinegar if necessary to create a sweet-tart chutney-like flavor. Spoon into a serving bowl; let cool completely.

2. Preheat oven to 400°F (200°C). Cut each pita in half crosswise, then carefully cut each piece in half horizontally to make 4 semi-circles from each pita. Cut each semi-circle into 3 wedges. Repeat procedure to make a total of 48 wedges. Place wedges smooth-side down on baking sheets. Spray lightly with baking spray; sprinkle lightly with remaining salt and pepper. Bake for 5 to 7 minutes or until crisp and starting to turn golden around the edges. Remove from baking sheet; cool completely on wire racks.

Kitchen Wisdom

To save time, prepare onions using a food processor fitted with a slicing disk.

Any leftover onion marmalade makes a fabulous topping for pizza; try it with fresh rosemary leaves and freshly grated Parmesan cheese. It's also wonderful in a sandwich with leftover roast chicken or roast beef.

3. Serve pâté on a lettuce-lined serving plate, along with a knife. Pile pita crisps in a napkin-lined basket, with the onion marmalade alongside.

Variation

In addition to salt and pepper, sprinkle pita chips before baking with any of the following: caraway, cumin, fennel or sesame seeds; chili or curry powder; dried basil, oregano, rosemary, tarragon or thyme.

Make Ahead

Onion marmalade can be refrigerated, covered, for up to 3 days. Pita crisps can be stored in an airtight container for up to 1 week.

Tandoori chicken with mango dip

Makes about 48 pieces; ¾ cup (175 mL) dip

Mild Indian spicing adds flavor to these low-fat chicken nuggets, while a yogurt marinade keeps them moist.

Kitchen Wisdom

When handling hot peppers, always wear rubber or plastic gloves and avoid touching your face. Wash your knife and cutting board in hot soapy water immediately afterward.

- Large nonreactive baking dish
- 2 baking sheets, lightly oiled

1	small onion, quartered	1
2	cloves garlic, sliced	2
1	1-inch (2.5 cm) piece ginger root, chopped	1
1	small hot pepper, seeded and chopped	1
1 cup	plain yogurt	250 mL
1 tsp	ground coriander	5 mL
½ tsp	ground cumin	2 mL
½ tsp	ground cardamom	2 mL
¼ tsp	ground mace	1 mL
¼ tsp	freshly grated nutmeg	1 mL
¼ tsp	ground cloves	1 mL
1½ lbs	boneless skinless chicken breasts, trimmed of excess fat and cut into 1-inch (2.5 cm) pieces	750 g

Mango Dip

¼ cup	mango chutney	50 mL
½ cup	plain yogurt	125 mL
	Lettuce leaves, lemon wedges and coriander sprigs	

1. In a food processor or blender, combine onion, garlic, ginger and hot pepper. Process until finely chopped and well combined. In the baking dish, stir together onion mixture, yogurt, coriander, cumin, cardamom, mace, nutmeg and cloves. Add chicken; toss to coat thoroughly. Refrigerate, covered, for at least 8 hours or up to 24 hours, stirring occasionally.

Kitchen Wisdom

Cardamom is a wonderfully aromatic spice used extensively in Indian cooking. Its mild flavor goes well with both savory and sweet dishes. Try a little cardamom in apple pie, rice pudding or any savory rice dish.

2. Preheat oven to 450°F (230°C). Remove chicken from marinade; shaking off any excess (discard marinade). On baking sheets, arrange chicken pieces in a single layer. Bake, turning once, for 10 to 12 minutes or until chicken is golden brown and no longer pink inside.

3. Mango Dip: If chutney has any large pieces of mango, mince them finely. In a serving bowl, stir together mango chutney and yogurt until smooth. Discard any dip that's left over after serving.

4. Arrange chicken on a lettuce-lined platter. Garnish with lemon wedges and coriander sprigs. Serve with mango dip alongside.

Make Ahead
Chicken should be marinated for at least 8 hours or up to 24 hours.

Spicy fried shrimp with maple-mustard dip

Serves 4 to 6

These shrimp take just minutes to make — a good thing because they're really addictive!

Kitchen Wisdom

Ground coriander comes from the seeds of the parsley-like plant we also know as cilantro. Ground coriander has an aromatic flavor and, although it isn't a hot spice, it's an essential ingredient in curries of all kinds.

Maple-Mustard Dip

¼ cup	mayonnaise	50 mL
1 tbsp	Dijon mustard	15 mL
1 tsp	maple syrup	5 mL
1 tsp	Worcestershire sauce	5 mL

Shrimp

1 tsp	salt	5 mL
1 tsp	ground coriander	5 mL
½ tsp	cayenne pepper	2 mL
½ tsp	ground cumin	2 mL
1 lb	raw large shrimp, peeled, deveined and patted dry	500 g
2 cups	canola oil or vegetable oil	500 mL
	Fresh coriander sprigs	

1. **Maple-Mustard Dip:** In a small serving bowl, combine mayonnaise, Dijon mustard, maple syrup and Worcestershire sauce; stir well. Refrigerate, covered, until ready to serve.

2. **Shrimp:** In a medium bowl, combine salt, coriander, cayenne and cumin. Add shrimp; toss well to coat evenly.

3. Preheat oven to 200°F (100°C). In a large deep skillet or in a Dutch oven, heat oil over medium-high heat. In batches fry shrimp, turning once, for 1 minute or until curled and pink. As each batch is ready, remove with a slotted spoon to a paper-towel-lined plate. Keep warm in oven until all shrimp are cooked.

4. To serve, pile shrimp in a napkin-lined basket. Garnish with sprigs of coriander. Serve at once with dip alongside. Discard any dip that's left over after serving.

> ### Make Ahead
> The dip can be refrigerated, covered, for up to 24 hours.

Red pepper and feta spread

Makes 1½ cups (375 mL)

I have a confession to make: I hate dips. They're messy, your guests have to huddle around a bowl and there's always the danger of someone committing the ultimate faux-pas of double dipping. A spread, on the other hand, serves the same purpose as a dip — but with much less angst for guests and host.

Serve this spread on crackers, melba toast or short lengths of celery.

• Baking sheet

1	red bell pepper	1
2 cups	crumbled feta cheese (about 8 oz/250 g)	500 mL
¼ tsp	hot pepper flakes	1 mL
	Fresh oregano or thyme sprigs or chopped fresh parsley	

1. Preheat broiler to high. Place red pepper on baking sheet. Broil, turning often, for 20 to 30 minutes or until skin is blackened and blistered. (Alternatively, cook pepper on barbecue over medium heat, turning often, for 15 to 20 minutes or until skin is blackened and blistered.) Transfer pepper to a plate; cover with a bowl and let stand for 10 minutes. Remove skin, seeds, stalk and any membrane from pepper; set aside until cool.

2. In a food processor, combine roasted pepper, feta cheese and hot pepper flakes; process until fairly smooth. Spoon into a serving bowl. Garnish with oregano, thyme or parsley.

> ### Make Ahead
> The spread can be refrigerated, covered, for up to 3 days.

Joe's gorgonzola-stuffed pears

Makes 24 pieces

These sensational stuffed pears were made by Joe Brancatella of Grazie Ristorante in Toronto for the opening of my friend Susan Meingast's art exhibit. I love them because they can be made in advance, are easy to eat and everyone seems to enjoy them.

Kitchen Wisdom

To make a delectable sit-down appetizer for 6, cut the stuffed pears into quarters and serve on a bed of Arugula and Boston Lettuce with Sherry Vinaigrette (see recipe, page 142), omitting the pine nuts.

3	firm ripe pears, washed and dried	3
	Freshly squeezed juice of 1 lemon	
4 oz	Gorgonzola cheese	125 g
	Lettuce leaves	

1. With a melon baller or small spoon, remove pear cores by hollowing them out from the wide base of each pear. Drizzle about 1 tsp (5 mL) lemon juice into each cavity, swirling to coat well. Shake excess juice back into bowl. Reserve remaining lemon juice.

2. In a small bowl, mash Gorgonzola cheese with a fork until fairly smooth. Pack cheese evenly into cavity of each pear. Wrap each pear tightly in plastic wrap. Refrigerate for at least 1 hour or up to 2 hours.

3. No more than 30 minutes before serving, unwrap pears. Using a large sharp knife (and wiping any cheese from knife with a damp cloth between cuts), cut each pear lengthwise into eighths. With a pastry brush, coat cut sides of each pear with reserved lemon juice. Arrange pear slices on a lettuce-lined serving platter. Serve at once.

> ### Make Ahead
> Refrigerate the stuffed pears for at least 1 hour or up to 2 hours.

Sit-down appetizers

See also...

Tomatoes and arugula with ricotta and basil oil

Serves 6

Michael Olson, now chef professor at the Niagara Culinary Institute, created this appetizer when he was chef of On The Twenty restaurant in Jordan, Ontario. It's the kind of deceptively simple yet intensely flavored dish that typifies Michael's cooking.

For the dressing, Michael uses grapeseed oil, which is mild-tasting and nutty-flavored. If unavailable, substitute olive oil.

Kitchen Wisdom

This salad is best prepared in late summer using fresh local tomatoes. At other times of the year, buy hothouse tomatoes (with stems intact) and let stand at room temperature for 5 to 7 days or until the stems are dry and the tomatoes are fully ripe. Never, ever refrigerate tomatoes or their texture will become woolly.

¾ cup	grapeseed oil or olive oil	175 mL
½ cup	packed fresh basil leaves	125 mL
2	beefsteak tomatoes or 3 hothouse tomatoes	2
8 cups	arugula, washed and dried, tough stems discarded and larger leaves torn into pieces	2 L
12 oz	regular (10%) ricotta cheese	375 g
½ tsp	black pepper	2 mL
¼ tsp	salt	1 mL

1. In a mini-chopper or food processor, combine oil and basil leaves. Process until well combined and basil is finely chopped. Refrigerate, covered, for 24 hours to allow the flavor to develop (do not store basil oil for longer than 24 hours).

2. Thirty minutes before serving, remove basil oil from refrigerator; let stand at room temperature.

3. Just before serving, scoop out tough stem ends from tomatoes with a small sharp knife; slice tomatoes thinly. Divide arugula among 6 dinner plates; arrange a circle of tomato slices on top of each portion. Spoon an equal amount of cheese in center of circle of tomatoes; sprinkle with pepper and salt. Whisk basil oil; drizzle about 2 tbsp (25 mL) over each serving. Serve at once.

> **Make Ahead**
> Basil oil must be refrigerated, covered, for 24 hours before serving.

Sizzling shrimp

Serves 6

This messy but delectable first course is perfect for sharing among good friends. Serve straight from the baking dish with good-quality crusty bread to mop up the spicy olive oil.

- 9-inch (22.5 cm) ovenproof earthenware dish or glass pie plate

1 1/2 lbs	raw large shrimp, peeled and deveined, patted dry	750 g
3	cloves garlic, sliced	3
1/4 tsp	salt	1 mL
1/4 tsp	hot pepper flakes	1 mL
1/2 cup	olive oil	125 mL

1. Preheat oven to 450°F (230°C). Spread out shrimp in baking dish; tuck slices of garlic in amongst shrimp. Sprinkle with salt and hot pepper flakes. Drizzle oil evenly over shrimp.

2. Bake for 10 to 12 minutes, stirring once or twice, until shrimp are pink and opaque and oil is bubbling. Serve at once.

Sautéed wild mushrooms on fresh greens

Serves 6

This simple appetizer takes very little time to prepare, although it must be served immediately. So follow it with something like Greek Swordfish with Tomatoes and Feta (see recipe, page 69), which needs little or no last-minute attention.

For best flavor, use a selection of fresh mushrooms.

Minus the salad greens and bread, the mushrooms can, of course, be served as an accompaniment, in which case they'd probably only stretch among 4 people.

Mesclun is a mix of different salad leaves, available in bulk in the produce section of most large supermarkets.

Encourage your guests to squeeze lemon wedges over mushrooms before eating.

Kitchen Wisdom

If you don't have a very large skillet, cook the mushrooms in 2 batches, adding the first batch back to the skillet once the second batch has reduced in volume.

½ oz	dried porcini mushrooms	15 g
	Boiling water	
⅓ cup	olive oil	75 mL
2 lbs	mixed fresh mushrooms (oyster, shiitake, portobello) wiped with damp paper towels and sliced thinly, tough stems discarded	1 kg
2	cloves garlic, minced	2
6 cups	mesclun or other salad greens, washed and dried, larger leaves torn into pieces	1.5 L
⅓ cup	chopped fresh parsley	75 mL
½ tsp	salt	2 mL
½ tsp	black pepper	2 mL
6	lemon wedges	6
1	baguette, thickly sliced	1

1. In a small heatproof bowl, cover porcini mushrooms with boiling water; let stand for 20 minutes. Drain well. Rinse under running water; drain. Chop coarsely; set aside.

2. In a large skillet, heat oil over medium-high heat. Add porcini mushrooms, fresh mushrooms and garlic. Cook, stirring occasionally, for 8 to 10 minutes or until mushrooms are tender and most of the juices have evaporated.

3. Meanwhile, divide mesclun among 6 individual plates. Add ¼ cup (50 mL) parsley, salt and pepper to mushrooms; spoon mushrooms evenly over mesclun. Sprinkle with remaining parsley; garnish each serving with a lemon wedge. Serve at once with sliced baguette.

Tomato and blue cheese tart

Serves 6

This easy appetizer would also make a perfect light lunch for 4 people, if served with a green salad. There's no need to remove the rind from the cheese.

• Baking sheet, lightly greased

Half	package (14 oz/397 g) frozen puff pastry, thawed	Half
6 oz	Cambazola, Gorgonzola or any other soft, mild blue cheese, thinly sliced	175 g
12	large fresh basil leaves	12
3	medium tomatoes, thinly sliced	3
$\frac{1}{2}$ tsp	black pepper	2 mL
1 tbsp	milk	15 mL
	Fresh basil leaves or mixed salad greens	

1. Preheat oven to 425°F (220°C). On a lightly floured surface, roll out pastry to a 12-inch (30 cm) square. Dampen edges of pastry; fold edges over to make a $\frac{1}{2}$-inch (1 cm) border all round. Lift pastry onto baking sheet.

2. Arrange cheese evenly over pastry; sprinkle with basil. Top evenly with overlapping rows of tomatoes; sprinkle with pepper. Brush edges of pastry with milk.

3. Bake for 20 to 25 minutes or until pastry is golden brown and cheese is bubbly. With a pizza wheel or sharp knife, cut tart into 6 rectangles. Serve warm, garnished with basil leaves or mixed salad greens.

Smoked fish Monte Carlo

Serves 6

I suspect this is an old classic recipe as I've spotted it on one or two menus in Britain, but I've yet to see it in a cookbook. It was a favorite supper dish of my late Uncle Trevor, but I think it also makes an elegant appetizer served in individual ramekins. The combination of smoky fish, nutty-tasting Gruyère cheese and fresh tomato is simply wonderful. The addition of dry mustard to any cheese sauce seems to bring out the flavor of the cheese, but you can omit it if it's unavailable. Serve the little pots of fish and sauce with thick slices of good-quality whole wheat bread.

- Six ¾-cup (175 mL) ovenproof ramekins or custard cups, lightly greased
- Baking sheet

1 lb	boneless smoked cod or haddock fillet or smoked mackerel fillets	500 g
2	medium tomatoes, cut in half crosswise	2
2 cups	cold milk	500 mL
¼ cup	butter, cut into pieces	50 mL
¼ cup	all-purpose flour	50 mL
½ tsp	dry mustard (optional)	2 mL
¼ tsp	black pepper	1 mL
1½ cups	shredded Gruyère cheese (about 5 oz/150 g)	375 mL
	Fresh parsley sprigs	

1. Preheat oven to 400°F (200°C). In a large deep skillet over high heat, cover cod with cold water; bring to a boil. Reduce heat to medium-low; simmer, uncovered, for 8 to 10 minutes or until cod flakes easily with a fork.

2. With a slotted spoon, remove cod from skillet; set aside. When cool enough to handle, break cod into small pieces with your fingers, discarding any skin and bones. Divide cod evenly among ramekins or custard cups.

3. Holding tomato halves over a bowl, squeeze gently to remove juice and seeds. Chop tomatoes finely, discarding tough stem ends. Divide tomatoes evenly among ramekins.

4. In a saucepan over medium-high heat, combine milk, butter, flour, mustard and pepper. Cook, whisking often, until milk is boiling and butter has melted. Reduce heat to medium-low; simmer, whisking constantly, for 2 to 3 minutes or until sauce has thickened and is smooth. Remove saucepan from heat; stir in 1 cup (250 mL) Gruyère cheese until melted and sauce is smooth.

5. Spoon sauce evenly over fish and tomatoes (ramekins will be very full). Sprinkle remaining Gruyère cheese evenly over top. Bake for 20 to 25 minutes or until sauce is bubbly and cheese has melted. If necessary, broil for 1 to 2 minutes or until tops turn golden brown. Remove ramekins from oven; let stand for 5 to 10 minutes. Serve garnished with parsley.

Make Ahead

Ramekins can be assembled and refrigerated, covered, for up to 24 hours. Bake as directed, adding 10 minutes to baking time.

Brewer's mussels

Serves 4 to 6

If you've enjoyed mussels in a restaurant, don't be put off cooking them at home because you think they're too complicated. They're surprisingly economical and much easier to prepare than you might think. In this recipe from Joe Brancatella, chef and co-owner of Grazie Ristorante in Toronto, the shellfish are steamed in beer (instead of the usual white wine), which gives them a mellow, hoppy flavor. Serve the mussels with some crusty bread to mop up the juices.

Kitchen Wisdom

Buy mussels — or any other shellfish for that matter — from a reputable fish store. And for greater ease, buy the cleaner cultured (not wild) mussels. When you get your mussels home, store them in a shallow dish in the refrigerator, covered with a damp tea towel, for up to 3 days.

3 lbs	mussels in their shells	1.5 kg
2 tbsp	olive oil	25 mL
2	cloves garlic, minced	2
1	bottle (12 oz/341 mL) pilsner-type beer	1
4	tomatoes, chopped	4
1/3 cup	chopped fresh parsley	75 mL
Half	lemon, thinly sliced lengthwise	Half
1/2 tsp	hot pepper flakes	2 mL
1/4 tsp	salt	1 mL
1/4 tsp	black pepper	1 mL

1. If using wild mussels, scrub to remove any mud or grit. If using cultured mussels, simply rinse under cold water. Using scissors, snip off beards (the scruffy-looking fringes poking out). Discard any mussels with open shells. If a shell is only slightly open, tap it lightly on the counter; keep mussels that close and discard those that remain open.

2. In a Dutch oven, heat oil over medium-high heat. Add garlic and cook, stirring, for 1 minute or until golden. Add beer, tomatoes, parsley, lemon slices, hot pepper flakes, salt and pepper. Increase heat to high; bring to a boil. Add mussels; reduce heat to medium-low. Simmer, covered, for 4 to 6 minutes or until mussels open. Discard any mussels that haven't opened after 6 minutes.

3. Divide mussels among 6 wide soup bowls. If desired, season cooking juices to taste with additional salt and pepper. Spoon cooking juices evenly over each portion of mussels, discarding lemon slices. Serve at once.

Clockwise from lower left:
Watermelon and Cherry-Tomato Brochettes (page 16); Red Pepper and Feta Spread (page 23); Tandoori Chicken with Mango Dip (page 20)

Mushroom and prosciutto antipasto with walnuts

Serves 4 to 6

Use the finest-quality, freshest walnuts you can find for this easy salad. It is best served within 2 hours of being made. Although it will taste fine the next day, the mushrooms tend to darken on standing.

Kitchen Wisdom

Since nuts go stale and rancid very quickly, it's best to buy them in small sealed packages from a store with a sufficiently fast turnover that you know they're fresh. If you're not going to use them immediately, store them in the freezer. For most recipes, you can use nuts straight from the freezer.

Use a sharp paring knife or vegetable peeler to shave a piece of fresh Parmesan cheese into thin flakes.

1 cup	walnut pieces (about 4 oz/125 g)	250 mL
3 cups	sliced button mushrooms (about 6 oz/175 g)	750 mL
¾ cup	shaved Parmesan cheese (about 2 oz/50 g)	175 mL
2 oz	prosciutto, trimmed of excess fat and chopped	50 g
¼ cup	fresh lemon juice	50 mL
2 tbsp	chopped fresh Italian flat-leafed parsley	25 mL
2 tbsp	olive oil	25 mL
¼ tsp	black pepper	1 mL
Pinch	salt (optional)	Pinch

1. In a small skillet over medium-high heat, toast walnuts, stirring often, for 3 to 5 minutes or until golden and fragrant. (Watch them carefully; they burn easily.) Remove from heat; let cool completely.

2. In a large serving bowl, stir together walnuts, mushrooms, Parmesan cheese and prosciutto. Sprinkle with lemon juice, parsley, olive oil and pepper; toss well. If desired, add salt and additional pepper. Serve at room temperature.

Nut-crusted scallops with mango salsa

Serves 6

This was one of the first menu items my good friend Arpi Magyar put on the menu of his Toronto restaurant Splendido Bar and Grill when it opened in 1991. Arpi coated the scallops in pistachio nuts and cooked them in the restaurant's ferociously hot pizza oven. However, using easier-to-find hazelnuts (filberts) and cranking a domestic oven up to 500°F (260°C) works just as well. Use fresh scallops for this recipe, since previously frozen ones are too moist to take the nut coating. Also, be sure not to overcook the scallops; they should only be just cooked in the center.

• Baking sheet with lightly oiled rack

Mango Salsa

2	ripe mangoes	2
1/3 cup	currants	75 mL
1	small jalapeño pepper, seeded and finely chopped	1
3 tbsp	fresh lemon juice	45 mL
1 tbsp	olive oil	15 mL

Scallops

1 cup	shelled hazelnuts	250 mL
1 tsp	fresh rosemary leaves	5 mL
1 tsp	fresh thyme leaves	5 mL
1/4 tsp	curry powder	1 mL
24	1 1/2-inch (4 cm) sea scallops (about 1 lb/500 g), patted dry	24
2 tbsp	vegetable oil	25 mL
2 cups	watercress, washed and dried, tough stems discarded	500 mL

1. **Mango Salsa:** Place 1 mango on the counter with its narrowest side uppermost. With a large sharp knife, slice down through mango, cutting each side away from pit and slicing as close to the pit as possible. With the point of a knife, cut a 1/2-inch (1 cm) crosshatch pattern in the flesh of the two pieces you have cut off. Turn slices "inside out;" cut the cubes of mango flesh away from skin. Cut the skin from the mango that remains around the pit; cut any remaining mango flesh from pit in 1/2-inch (1 cm) cubes. Repeat with remaining mango. Put mango cubes in a medium bowl. Stir in currants, jalapeño pepper, lemon juice and olive oil. Let stand at room temperature for 1 hour to allow flavors to blend.

When handling hot peppers, always wear rubber or plastic gloves and avoid touching your face. Wash your knife and cutting board in hot soapy water immediately afterward.

Mangoes are ripe when they are fragrant and yield slightly to gentle pressure.

2. **Scallops:** In a small skillet over medium-high heat, toast hazelnuts, stirring often, for 3 to 5 minutes or until they start to darken and are fragrant. (Watch them carefully; they burn easily). Remove from heat and transfer to a clean tea towel; wrap nuts completely and rub vigorously to remove skins.

3. In a food processor, combine hazelnuts, rosemary, thyme and curry powder; process until nuts are finely chopped. (Don't overprocess or nuts will become oily.) Transfer hazelnut mixture to a shallow dish.

4. Brush scallops on both sides with oil. Toss each scallop in hazelnut mixture to coat completely; place scallops on rack on baking sheet. Just before serving, preheat oven to 500°F (260°C). Bake scallops for 5 to 7 minutes or until hazelnuts begin to brown and scallops are opaque.

5. Divide watercress among 6 individual plates; arrange 4 scallops on each plate. Spoon some mango salsa in center of each plate. Serve at once.

Make Ahead
Scallops can be coated with the nut mixture then refrigerated, covered, for up to 4 hours. Salsa can be refrigerated, covered, for up to 24 hours. Let stand at room temperature for 30 minutes before serving.

Lentil and pancetta antipasto

Serves 6

Pancetta is Italian bacon cured with nutmeg, cinnamon or cloves to give it a distinctive flavor. If pancetta is unavailable, regular bacon can be substituted, but the flavor won't be as authentically Italian.

Kitchen Wisdom

For a colorful antipasti platter to serve as a sit-down appetizer, spoon this salad onto a platter, along with Mushroom and Prosciutto Antipasto with Walnuts (see recipe, page 33), a couple of tomatoes cut into wedges, a selection of olives and some sliced mozzarella or bocconcini cheese.

1 cup	green lentils	250 mL
4	sprigs fresh oregano or marjoram	4
2 oz	pancetta, chopped	50 g
2	stalks celery, finely chopped	2
Half	medium red onion, finely chopped	Half
1/4 cup	chopped fresh Italian flat-leafed parsley	50 mL
1	clove garlic, minced	1
2 tbsp	olive oil	25 mL
1 tbsp	chopped fresh oregano or marjoram	15 mL
1 tbsp	red wine vinegar	15 mL
1/2 tsp	black pepper	2 mL
1/4 tsp	salt	1 mL

1. Rinse lentils under running water, picking them over and discarding any grit. Drain well. Bring a medium saucepan of water to boil over high heat. Add lentils and oregano sprigs; cook, uncovered, for 15 to 20 minutes or until lentils are tender but still firm. Drain well, discarding oregano; transfer lentils to a large serving bowl.

2. In a small heavy skillet, cook pancetta over medium-high heat for 2 to 3 minutes or until just starting to crisp. With a slotted spoon, remove pancetta from skillet; drain on a paper-towel-lined plate.

3. Add pancetta, celery, onion, parsley and garlic to lentils; toss well. Sprinkle with oil, oregano, vinegar, pepper and salt; toss well. If desired, season to taste with additional salt and pepper. Serve at room temperature.

> ### Make Ahead
> Antipasto can be refrigerated, covered, for up to 24 hours. Let stand at room temperature for 30 minutes before serving.

Soups

See also...

Roasted red pepper and garlic soup

Serves 6

Food writer Kathleen Sloan, is famous for her Thanksgiving dinners. One year, she concocted this delicious soup to use up leftover peppers. It's rich without being heavy and the peppers take on a lovely smoky flavor after roasting.

• Shallow roasting pan

2	whole heads garlic	2
4	red bell peppers	4
1	large onion, cut into quarters	1
5 cups	chicken stock	1.25 L
4	large sprigs fresh thyme (or 1/2 tsp/2 mL dried)	4
1/4 tsp	salt	1 mL
1/4 tsp	black pepper	1 mL
Pinch	hot pepper flakes	Pinch
1/4 cup	dry sherry (optional)	50 mL
1/4 cup	whipping (35%) cream	50 mL
1/4 cup	plain yogurt	50 mL
6	tiny sprigs fresh thyme	6

1. Preheat oven to 400°F (200°C). Cut a slice off the top of each head of garlic so the tops of cloves are exposed. Put garlic, red peppers and onion in roasting pan. Roast, turning peppers and onion occasionally, for 40 to 50 minutes or until vegetables are tender. Remove from oven; set onion and garlic aside. Place peppers on a plate and cover with a bowl; let stand for 10 minutes.

2. When cool enough to handle, remove skin, seeds, stalk and any membrane from peppers; transfer flesh to a large saucepan. With the tip of a knife or small spoon, scoop softened cloves from roasted garlic heads. Add to saucepan along with roasted onion, stock, thyme, salt, pepper and hot pepper flakes. Bring mixture to a boil. Reduce heat to medium-low; simmer, covered, for 20 minutes. If using fresh thyme, discard sprigs.

Kitchen Wisdom

Although dry sherry may not be your favorite tipple, it's handy to have tucked away in the refrigerator. A dash added to a soup, sauce or stew can give it special-occasion status. Many Asian dishes, including stir-fries, are also improved with a little sherry.

3. In a blender, purée soup in batches until smooth. Pour through a fine sieve into rinsed-out saucepan, pressing on solids to extract as much liquid as possible. Stir in sherry and cream. Heat soup over medium heat until piping hot (but not boiling). If desired, season to taste with additional salt and pepper. Ladle into 6 warm soup bowls. Swirl a spoonful of yogurt into each serving; garnish each with a tiny sprig of fresh thyme. Serve at once.

Make Ahead

The peppers, garlic and onion can be roasted then refrigerated, covered, for up to 24 hours. The finished soup can be refrigerated, covered, for up to 3 days. Reheat over medium heat until piping hot, but do not allow to boil.

Thai-style chicken and coconut soup

Serves 6

This is a kind of pretend Thai soup, but it's still full of flavor and surprisingly quick to make. Its spiciness seems to be welcome whatever the season, but the soup is especially comforting when chill winds are blowing outside.

1 tbsp	canola oil or vegetable oil	15 mL
1	onion, finely chopped	1
1 tbsp	minced ginger root	15 mL
$1/4$ tsp	minced fresh hot chili or pinch hot pepper flakes	1 mL
4 cups	chicken stock	1 L
2 tbsp	fresh lime juice	25 mL
2 tsp	grated lime zest	10 mL
$1/4$ tsp	salt	1 mL
2	boneless skinless chicken breasts, trimmed of excess fat	2
1	can (14 oz/398 mL) unsweetened coconut milk	1
$1/3$ cup	finely chopped fresh coriander	75 mL

1. In a large saucepan, heat oil over medium-high heat. Add onion, ginger and chili; cook, stirring, for 3 to 5 minutes or until onion is soft but not brown. Add chicken stock, lime juice, lime zest and salt, stirring to combine well. Increase heat to high; bring mixture to a boil.

2. Add chicken breasts. Reduce heat to medium-low; simmer, covered and turning once, for 10 to 15 minutes or until chicken is no longer pink inside. Remove from heat. Using tongs, transfer chicken to a plate and allow to cool slightly; when cool enough to handle, cut into $1/2$-inch (1 cm) pieces.

3. Return chicken to soup. Stir in coconut milk and coriander. Cook, stirring constantly, over medium heat until piping hot. (Do not allow to boil or soup will curdle.) If desired, season to taste with additional salt and pepper. Ladle into warm soup bowls; serve at once.

> **Make Ahead**
> Soup can be refrigerated, covered, for up to 24 hours. Reheat over medium heat until piping hot, but do not allow to boil.

Herbaceous soup

Serves 6

You can vary the flavor of this soup according to the herbs you choose. Use soft-leafed varieties such as dill, basil, tarragon, mint, sage, oregano, parsley and chives — in any combination. Avoid tougher varieties such as rosemary and thyme.

Potatoes give this soup a creamy texture and eliminate the need for cream or other high-fat ingredients.

Kitchen Wisdom

To clean leeks, slit them open lengthwise, but do not cut right through. Hold leeks under cold running water, opening them up slightly to wash away grit. Shake leeks to remove excess water.

For a silky-smooth result when puréeing soups, always use a blender rather than a food processor.

2 tbsp	butter	25 mL
4	medium leeks (white and light green parts only), trimmed, washed and thinly sliced	4
8 cups	chicken stock	2 L
4	medium potatoes, peeled and cut into 1/2-inch (1 cm) pieces	4
1/4 tsp	salt	1 mL
1/4 tsp	black pepper	1 mL
1 cup	packed fresh herbs, stems discarded (see note at left, for suggestions)	250 mL
1/4 cup	goat cheese or cream cheese, softened	50 mL
6	fresh herb sprigs or 2 tbsp (25 mL) snipped fresh chives	6

1. In a large saucepan, heat butter over medium heat. Add leeks; cook, stirring, for 3 to 5 minutes or until soft but not brown. Add stock, potatoes, salt and pepper; bring to a boil over high heat. Reduce heat to low; simmer, covered, for 15 to 20 minutes or until potatoes are tender. Stir in herbs; simmer for 5 minutes.

2. In a blender, purée soup in batches until smooth. Return soup to rinsed-out saucepan. Heat over medium-high heat until soup is piping hot (but not boiling). If desired, season to taste with additional salt and pepper.

3. Ladle into warm soup bowls. Top each portion with a spoonful of goat cheese and a sprig of fresh herbs. Serve at once.

Moroccan spiced lentil soup

Serves 6

Most Mediterranean countries have their own version of this satisfying soup — a wonderful concoction of legumes, herbs and spices. Here's how it's made in North Africa. Serve with focaccia or pita bread and follow it with a lighter main course, such as Lemon Roast Chicken Thighs (see recipe, page 88).

1 tbsp	olive oil	15 mL
2	onions, chopped	2
1	clove garlic, minced	1
1 tsp	ground ginger	5 mL
1 tsp	paprika	5 mL
1 tsp	turmeric	5 mL
1/4 tsp	cayenne pepper	1 mL
1 cup	red lentils, rinsed and drained	250 mL
4 cups	beef stock or chicken stock	1 L
1	can (28 oz/796 mL) diced tomatoes	1
1	can (19 oz/540 mL) chickpeas, rinsed and drained	1
1/3 cup	chopped fresh coriander	75 mL
1/4 tsp	salt	1 mL
1/4 tsp	black pepper	1 mL

1. In a large saucepan or Dutch oven, heat oil over medium-high heat. Add onions and garlic; cook, stirring, for 3 to 5 minutes or until onions are soft but not brown. Add ginger, paprika, turmeric and cayenne; cook, stirring, for about 1 minute. Add lentils; stir to coat with onion-and-spice mixture.

2. Add stock and tomatoes. Bring to a boil over high heat, stirring occasionally. Reduce heat to medium-low; simmer, covered, for 30 to 40 minutes or until lentils are very soft and have started to break up.

3. Stir in chickpeas, coriander, salt and pepper; simmer, uncovered, for 10 minutes to allow flavors to blend. If desired, season to taste with additional salt and pepper. Ladle into warm soup bowls. Serve at once.

> **Make Ahead**
> Soup can be refrigerated, covered, for up to 3 days. Reheat over medium heat until piping hot, adding a little extra stock if soup has become too thick.

Shrimp broth with coriander

Serves 6

Dinner guests always seem to enjoy the drama of having something cooked at the table. In this simple but exquisite recipe, chopped shrimp cook almost instantly when boiling stock is poured over them. (Of course, if such theatrics are not to your taste, you can always add the stock in the kitchen and carry the finished soup to the table.)

I first enjoyed a version of this soup at a restaurant called Yung Kee in Hong Kong. Yung Kee's chef used lobster meat but it's just as delicious — and a little easier to prepare — using shrimp.

1 lb	raw large shrimp, shelled and deveined, shells reserved	500 g
8 cups	chicken stock or fish stock	2 L
1/4 cup	chopped green onions	50 mL
1	clove garlic, peeled but left whole	1
1	1-inch (2.5 cm) piece ginger root, thinly sliced	1
2	2-inch (5 cm) strips lemon zest	2
1 tsp	whole black peppercorns	5 mL
2 or 3	large sprigs fresh coriander	2 or 3
1/3 cup	chopped fresh coriander	75 mL

1. Cut shrimp crosswise into 1/4-inch (5 mm) pieces; refrigerate, covered, until ready to serve.

2. In a large saucepan over high heat, combine shrimp shells, stock, green onions, garlic, ginger, lemon zest, peppercorns and coriander sprigs; bring to a boil. Reduce heat to low; simmer gently, covered, for 1 hour. Strain stock through a fine sieve into a 3-cup (750 mL) pitcher; discard flavorings.

3. When ready to serve, warm a 10-cup (2.5 L) soup tureen or serving bowl. Pour stock into a large saucepan; bring to a full rolling boil over high heat. Place shrimp and chopped coriander in soup tureen. At the table, pour boiling stock into soup tureen; stir once or twice. When shrimp are pink and firm, ladle soup into warm soup bowls. Serve at once.

Make Ahead
Shrimp can be shelled, chopped and refrigerated, covered, for up to 24 hours.

Stock can be boiled with flavorings, then strained and refrigerated, covered, for up to 24 hours.

Roasted parsnip soup with turmeric swirl

Serves 6

Roasting parsnips brings out their natural sweetness which, in turn, teams well with spicy flavors. There's just a touch of curry in this creamy soup, so it's not too hot — just wonderfully comforting. Toasting the turmeric before adding it to the yogurt eliminates any raw taste the spice might have.

• Large shallow roasting pan

2 lbs	parsnips, peeled, trimmed and cut into 1- by ½-inch (2.5 by 1 cm) pieces	1 kg
2 tbsp	canola oil or vegetable oil	25 mL
½ tsp	salt	2 mL
½ tsp	black pepper	2 mL
1	onion, finely chopped	1
2	cloves garlic, minced	2
1 tsp	curry powder (mild or medium)	5 mL
6 to 7 cups	chicken stock	1.5 to 1.75 L
1 tsp	turmeric	5 mL
½ cup	plain yogurt	125 mL
¼ cup	chopped fresh coriander	50 mL
6	fresh coriander sprigs	6

1. Preheat oven to 400°F (200°C). In roasting pan, combine parsnips, 1 tbsp (15 mL) oil, ¼ tsp (1 mL) salt and ¼ tsp (1 mL) black pepper; toss well. Roast, uncovered and stirring occasionally, for 40 to 45 minutes or until parsnips are tender and golden brown. Set aside.

2. In a large saucepan or Dutch oven, heat remaining oil over medium-high heat. Add onion; cook, stirring, for 3 to 5 minutes or until onion is soft but not brown. Add garlic and curry powder; cook, stirring, for 2 to 3 minutes or until fragrant. (Do not let garlic brown.) Add parsnips, 6 cups (1.5 L) stock and remaining salt and pepper. Bring to a boil over high heat. Reduce heat to medium-low; simmer, covered, for 20 to 30 minutes or until all vegetables are tender.

Kitchen Wisdom

Turmeric is a bright yellow spice that adds a mild aroma and distinctive color to all kinds of dishes. It is made from the dried rhizome of a plant related to ginger and appears often in Indian and Pakistani recipes.

3. Meanwhile, in a small dry skillet, toast turmeric over medium heat, stirring often, for 1 to 2 minutes or until turmeric darkens slightly, smells aromatic and starts to smoke. Remove from heat; scrape into a bowl and let cool completely. Add yogurt; stir well. Set aside.

4. In a blender, purée soup in batches until smooth. Return soup to rinsed-out saucepan; if soup is too thick, add remaining 1 cup (250 mL) stock. Stir in chopped coriander. Reheat soup over medium heat until piping hot (but not boiling). If desired, season to taste with additional salt and pepper. Ladle into warm soup bowls. Swirl a spoonful of turmeric-flavored yogurt into each serving. Garnish with coriander sprigs. Serve at once.

> ### Make Ahead
> Soup can be refrigerated, covered, for up to 3 days. Reheat over medium heat until piping hot, but do not allow to boil.

Chunky Bermudan fish chowder

Serves 6 to 8

On the island of Bermuda, fish chowder is traditionally a dark-colored, homogenous mixture that is cooked for hours. I love the flavor but am not keen on the texture, preferring a chunkier-style soup. So I'll confess that here I've taken some real liberties with the original.

After a recent trip to Bermuda, my good friends Brian and Dana-Marie Langley brought me back a recipe from Bermudan condiment manufacturer Outerbridge Peppers Ltd. With thanks to Outerbridge, here's my version.

Kitchen Wisdom

To speed up preparation time, use a food processor to chop the vegetables.

2 tbsp	canola oil or vegetable oil	25 mL
1	large onion, finely chopped	1
1	clove garlic, minced	1
2	large potatoes, peeled and finely chopped	2
2	large carrots, peeled and finely chopped	2
1 cup	finely chopped celery	250 mL
1	green or red bell pepper, seeded and finely chopped	1
2 tsp	dried thyme	10 mL
1/4 tsp	salt	1 mL
1/4 tsp	black pepper	1 mL
1/4 tsp	ground cloves	1 mL
1	bay leaf	1
1	can (10 oz/284 mL) low-sodium beef broth	1
1	can (28 oz/796 mL) diced tomatoes	1
1/4 cup	ketchup	50 mL
1/4 cup	dark or amber rum	50 mL
1 tbsp	Worcestershire sauce	15 mL
1 lb	boneless, skinless red snapper or Boston bluefish fillets, finely chopped or frozen fish fillets, thawed and finely chopped	500 g
1/2 cup	chopped fresh parsley	125 mL
	Hot pepper sauce	

1. In a large saucepan or Dutch oven, heat oil over medium-high heat. Add onion and garlic; cook, stirring, for 3 to 5 minutes or until onion is soft but not brown. Add potatoes, carrots, celery, bell pepper, thyme, salt, pepper, cloves and bay leaf. Cook, stirring, for 3 to 5 minutes or until bell pepper starts to soften.

Kitchen Wisdom

When preparing celery, don't remove individual stalks — use the whole bunch, slicing it as you need it, starting from the leafy tops. Keeping the root end intact this way helps the celery stay fresh longer.

A miniature bottle of rum (airline size) contains the $\frac{1}{4}$ cup (50 mL) needed for this recipe.

2. Stir in canned beef broth and 1 can water; bring to a boil over high heat. Reduce heat to medium-low; simmer, covered, for 15 minutes or until vegetables are just tender.

3. Stir in tomatoes, ketchup, rum and Worcestershire sauce; bring to a boil over high heat. Reduce heat to medium-low; simmer, covered, for 1 hour or until vegetables are very tender.

4. Stir in fish; simmer, covered, for 10 minutes or until fish is opaque. Stir in parsley; season to taste with additional salt and pepper. Ladle into warm soup bowls. Serve at once with hot pepper sauce.

Make Ahead
Chowder can be refrigerated, covered, for up to 2 days. Reheat over medium heat until piping hot, but do not allow to boil.

Neon beet soup

Serves 6

This dazzling pink soup looks simply stunning if you serve it in white soup bowls. Although I can barely believe it now, during my "punk" phase in the 1970s, I actually had my hairdresser streak my hair this color. Go figure.

Kitchen Wisdom

For a silky-smooth result when puréeing soups, always use a blender rather than a food processor.

Make Ahead
Soup can be refrigerated, covered, for up to 3 days. Reheat over medium heat until piping hot, but do not allow to boil.

• Shallow baking dish

1 lb	beets, scrubbed	500 g
1 tbsp	canola oil or vegetable oil	15 mL
1	onion, chopped	1
1	clove garlic, minced	1
1	can (28 oz/796 mL) diced tomatoes	1
2 cups	chicken stock	500 mL
1/3 cup	chopped fresh dill	75 mL
1 tbsp	maple syrup or liquid honey or brown sugar	15 mL
1/4 tsp	salt	1 mL
1/4 tsp	black pepper	1 mL
1/3 cup	sour cream	75 mL

1. Preheat oven to 400°F (200°C). Trim off all but 1 inch (2.5 cm) of stems from beets. Place beets in baking dish. Add water to a depth of 1/2 inch (1 cm). Bake, tightly covered, for 1 1/2 hours or until beets are tender. Remove from oven; uncover and let stand until cool enough to handle.

2. In a large saucepan, heat oil over medium-high heat. Add onion and garlic; cook, stirring, for 3 to 5 minutes or until onion is soft but not brown. Remove from heat.

3. Peel skins from beets; cut into 1-inch (2.5 cm) pieces. In a blender combine, in batches, onion mixture, beets and tomatoes; purée until smooth. Pour soup back into saucepan as each batch is blended.

4. Add chicken stock, 1/4 cup (50 mL) dill, maple syrup, salt and pepper. Bring to a boil. Reduce heat to medium-low; simmer, stirring occasionally, for 5 minutes. If desired, season to taste with additional salt and pepper. Ladle into warm soup bowls. Swirl a spoonful of sour cream into each portion. Sprinkle with remaining dill; serve at once.

Pasta and breads

Farfalle with roasted squash and garlic cream

Serves 6

Here's an example of how a humble winter vegetable like squash can be transformed into an elegant meal. Serve this rich dish with a simple green salad such as Arugula and Boston Lettuce with Sherry Vinaigrette and Pine Nuts (see recipe, page 142) plus good-quality bread on the side. Don't be alarmed at the amount of garlic in this recipe — roasting renders it sweet and mild.

Kitchen Wisdom

Farfalle is pasta shaped like bow ties. If unavailable, substitute rotini or penne.

Use a sharp vegetable peeler to peel the squash.

• Large shallow roasting pan

3 lbs	butternut or acorn squash, peeled, seeds removed and cut into ½-inch (1 cm) cubes	1.5 kg
3 tbsp	olive oil	45 mL
½ tsp	salt	2 mL
½ tsp	black pepper	2 mL
2	whole heads garlic, tops sliced off	2
1 cup	whipping (35%) cream	250 mL
½ cup	chopped green onions	125 mL
¼ tsp	freshly grated nutmeg	1 mL
1 lb	farfalle (bow-tie pasta)	500 g
¼ cup	chopped fresh parsley	50 mL
	Freshly grated Parmesan cheese	

1. Preheat oven to 400°F (200°C). In the roasting pan, toss squash with all but 2 tsp (10 mL) oil. Sprinkle with ¼ tsp (1 mL) each salt and pepper; toss well. Add garlic, cut-sides up; drizzle with remaining oil. Roast, stirring squash occasionally, for 30 to 35 minutes or until squash and garlic are tender. Remove from oven; set aside to cool.

2. When cool enough to handle, scoop softened cloves from garlic heads with tip of a knife or a small spoon. In a small bowl, mash garlic with back of a spoon until smooth.

3. In a small saucepan over medium-high heat, whisk together garlic, whipping cream, green onions, nutmeg and remaining salt and pepper; bring to a boil. Reduce heat to low; keep warm, stirring occasionally.

For best flavor, always grate your own nutmeg. Whole nutmegs will last for years if stored in a sealed jar in a dark cupboard; ready-grated nutmeg goes stale very quickly.

4. Meanwhile, in a large pot of boiling salted water, cook pasta for 8 to 10 minutes or until tender but firm. Drain well in a colander but do not rinse. Return pasta to pot over low heat. Add squash and any oil and cooking juices remaining in roasting pan, garlic cream and parsley. Stir gently until pasta is coated with sauce, taking care not to break up squash pieces. If desired, season to taste with additional salt and pepper. Serve at once in warm pasta bowls; sprinkle with Parmesan cheese.

Make Ahead
Squash can be roasted then refrigerated, covered, for up to 24 hours. Garlic cream can be refrigerated, covered, for up to 24 hours.

Speedy focaccia

Serves 6

Focaccia, a delicious flatbread from the Genoa region of Italy, is perfect as an accompaniment to any main course, or teamed with pâté or cheese for an appetizer. Focaccia is time-consuming to prepare from scratch, but a good version can be made in double-quick time from ready-made pizza dough.

• Baking sheet, lightly oiled

1 lb	ready-made unbaked pizza dough, thawed if frozen and cut in half	500 g
	Toppings (see facing page)	
2 tbsp	olive oil	25 mL

1. Preheat oven to 450°F (230°C). On a lightly floured surface, knead each piece of dough to expel any pockets of air. Roll out each piece to a 10- by 6-inch (25 by 15 cm) oval. Place dough on baking sheet.

2. With fingers, make indents over each piece of dough. Add topping of your choice; drizzle each piece of dough with 1 tbsp (15 mL) olive oil. Bake for 18 to 20 minutes or until focaccia are puffy and golden brown. Slide focaccia onto wire rack; cool slightly. Cut each into 3 pieces; serve warm.

If using frozen pizza
dough, thaw in
refrigerator for 8 hours
before rolling out.

Toppings

Classic Rosemary
2 tsp (10 mL) minced fresh rosemary leaves

$\frac{1}{2}$ tsp (2 mL) coarse salt

$\frac{1}{4}$ tsp (1 mL) black pepper

Tomato-Fennel
$\frac{1}{4}$ cup (50 mL) finely chopped tomato

1 tsp (5 mL) fennel seeds

$\frac{1}{4}$ tsp (1 mL) black pepper

Leek-Parmesan
$\frac{1}{4}$ cup (50 mL) thinly sliced leeks
(white and light green parts only)

2 tbsp (25 mL) freshly grated Parmesan cheese

$\frac{1}{4}$ tsp (1 mL) black pepper

Pesto and Mushroom
2 tbsp (25 mL) pesto sauce

$\frac{1}{2}$ cup (125 mL) finely chopped mushrooms

Spaghetti with pancetta and gorgonzola

Serves 4 to 6

This quick-fix dish combines two of my favorite ingredients — Gorgonzola and arugula — in a creamy pasta sauce that's perfect for a casual dinner.

Kitchen Wisdom

Pancetta is Italian bacon cured with nutmeg, cinnamon or cloves to give it a distinctive flavor. Look for it in the deli section of most large supermarkets. If pancetta is unavailable, substitute regular bacon.

1 lb	spaghetti	500 g
6 oz	pancetta, chopped	175 g
6 cups	arugula or watercress, washed, dried, tough stems discarded and larger leaves torn into pieces	1.5 L
1	clove garlic, minced	1
6 oz	Gorgonzola cheese, crumbled	175 g
2/3 cup	sour cream	150 mL
1/4 cup	chopped fresh parsley	50 mL
1/2 tsp	black pepper	2 mL
Pinch	salt (optional)	Pinch

1. In a large pot of boiling salted water, cook spaghetti for 8 to 10 minutes or until tender but firm.

2. Meanwhile, in a large skillet over medium-high heat, cook pancetta for 3 to 5 minutes or until crisp. If necessary, drain off all but 1 tbsp (15 mL) fat from skillet. (You may only have excess fat if you use regular bacon.) Add arugula and garlic; cook, stirring, for 1 minute or until arugula is wilted. Remove skillet from heat.

3. Drain spaghetti in a colander but do not rinse; return to pot over low heat. Add pancetta-arugula mixture, along with Gorgonzola, sour cream, parsley and pepper. Toss gently until cheese is melted and sauce is hot. If desired, season to taste with salt and additional pepper. Serve at once in warm pasta bowls.

Linguine with puttanesca sauce

Serves 4

This classic recipe comes from my good friend, food professional Carolyn Gall-Casey, who says it's one of her favorite choices for entertaining. And no wonder — the spicy sauce uses ingredients you probably have in your cupboard and can be made ahead of time. Incidentally, Carolyn says the devilishly good sauce was named for Italy's ladies of the night, the intense flavors of the sauce apparently suiting their adventuresome palates!

Kitchen Wisdom

Capers are the pickled flower buds of a bush that grows in the Mediterranean region. They have a distinctive, pleasantly astringent flavor. Look for them in the pickle section of your supermarket.

If ground tomatoes are unavailable, use a 28-oz (796 mL) can of regular tomatoes. In a food processor, process tomatoes with their juice using on-off pulses until fairly smooth.

Always buy good-quality pasta. It may cost a little extra but the superior texture and flavor is worth it.

2 tbsp	olive oil	25 mL
½ cup	sliced pitted kalamata olives	125 mL
½ cup	sliced pitted green olives	125 mL
4	cloves garlic, minced	4
2 tbsp	drained capers	25 mL
1 tsp	anchovy paste	5 mL
¼ to ½ tsp	hot pepper flakes	1 to 2 mL
¼ tsp	salt	1 mL
¼ tsp	dried oregano	1 mL
1	can (28 oz/796 mL) ground tomatoes	1
1 lb	linguine	500 g
¼ cup	chopped fresh Italian flat-leafed parsley	50 mL
	Freshly grated Parmesan cheese	

1. In a large skillet, heat oil over medium heat. Add kalamata olives, green olives, garlic, capers, anchovy paste, hot pepper flakes, salt and oregano. Cook, stirring, for 2 to 3 minutes or until garlic is soft and mixture is fragrant. Stir in tomatoes; bring to a boil. Reduce heat to medium-low; simmer, uncovered and stirring occasionally, for 15 to 20 minutes or until most of the liquid has evaporated.

2. Meanwhile, in a large pot of boiling salted water, cook linguine for 8 to 10 minutes or until tender but firm. Drain in a colander but do not rinse; return pasta to pot. Add sauce and parsley; toss until well coated. Serve at once in warm pasta bowls accompanied by Parmesan cheese for sprinkling on top.

> ### Make Ahead
> The sauce can be refrigerated, covered, for up to 24 hours. Reheat in a skillet over medium-low heat until bubbly or microwave on High for 3 to 5 minutes, stirring occasionally.

Chicken and fusilli bake with ricotta topping

Serves 6 to 8

I love lasagna but hate preparing it. Life's just too short to be juggling hot, slippery ribbons of pasta. And I always seem to get the layering wrong — too much here, not enough there. This baked pasta dish delivers all the flavor of a good lasagna without the hassle.

Don't be tempted to use light (5%) ricotta cheese in the topping; it may curdle.

- 10-cup (2.5 L) baking dish, greased
- Baking sheet lined with foil

2 tbsp	olive oil	25 mL
1	large onion, chopped	1
1	yellow or green bell pepper, seeded and chopped	1
2	cloves garlic, minced	2
1	can (28 oz/796 mL) diced tomatoes	1
1/4 cup	tomato paste	50 mL
1/2 tsp	salt	2 mL
1/2 tsp	dried basil	2 mL
1/4 tsp	black pepper	1 mL
1/4 tsp	hot pepper flakes	1 mL
1	bay leaf	1
1 lb	skinless boneless chicken breasts, cut into 1/2-inch (1 cm) pieces	500 g
1/4 cup	chopped fresh parsley	50 mL
3 cups	fusilli (spiral pasta)	750 mL

Topping

1	container (1 lb/500 g) regular (10%) ricotta cheese	1
2	eggs, lightly beaten	2
1/4 tsp	salt	1 mL
1/4 tsp	black pepper	1 mL
1/4 tsp	freshly grated nutmeg	1 mL
1/2 cup	freshly grated Parmesan cheese	125 mL

If you have any leftover cooked chicken in the fridge, use 2 cups (500 mL) cubed chicken in place of the chicken breasts. Add it to the tomato sauce when you add parsley.

1. In a large saucepan or Dutch oven, heat oil over medium-high heat. Add onion, bell pepper and garlic; cook, stirring, for 3 to 5 minutes or until onion is soft but not brown. Stir in tomatoes, tomato paste, salt, basil, black pepper, hot pepper flakes and bay leaf; bring to a boil over high heat. Reduce heat to medium-low; simmer, covered, for 15 minutes. Add chicken and cook, covered, for 5 to 7 minutes or until chicken is no longer pink inside. Stir in parsley; remove saucepan from heat. Discard bay leaf.

2. Meanwhile, in a large pot of boiling salted water, cook fusilli for 8 to 10 minutes or until tender but firm. Drain well in a colander but do not rinse.

3. Preheat oven to 350°F (180°C). In prepared baking dish, layer half the fusilli. Add chicken mixture; top with remaining fusilli.

4. **Topping:** In a medium bowl, stir together ricotta cheese, eggs, salt, pepper and nutmeg. Spoon mixture evenly over top layer of fusilli, covering completely. Sprinkle with Parmesan cheese. Bake, uncovered, for 35 to 40 minutes or until mixture is bubbly and top is puffy and golden brown. Remove from oven; let stand for 10 minutes before serving.

Make Ahead
The pasta can be assembled then refrigerated, covered, for up to 24 hours. Let stand at room temperature for 30 minutes, then bake as directed in the recipe.

Penne with roasted eggplant and wild mushrooms

Serves 6

To ensure the best texture and taste for this easy pasta sauce, choose a selection of fresh mushrooms such as sliced oyster or shiitake (discard stems before using) or chopped portobello. The dried porcini mushrooms add an intense woodsy flavor; look for them in the produce section of most large supermarkets.

If porcini mushrooms are unavailable, look for dried chanterelles.

• Shallow roasting pan

1 cup	boiling water	250 mL
1/2 oz	dried porcini mushrooms	15 g
1	large eggplant, trimmed and cut into 1/2-inch (1 cm) cubes	1
1/4 cup	olive oil	50 mL
1/2 tsp	salt	2 mL
1/2 tsp	black pepper	2 mL
1 lb	penne or rotini	500 g
2 cups	sliced fresh mushrooms (about 8 oz/250 g) (see note at left)	500 mL
4 oz	prosciutto, trimmed of excess fat and coarsely chopped	125 g
1	clove garlic, minced	1
2 tsp	minced fresh rosemary leaves (or 1 tsp/5 mL crumbled dried)	10 mL
1 cup	regular (10%) or light (5%) ricotta cheese	250 mL
	Fresh rosemary sprigs	

1. Preheat oven to 425°F (220°C). In a small heatproof bowl, combine boiling water and porcini mushrooms; let stand for 20 minutes.

2. In the roasting pan, combine eggplant, 3 tbsp (45 mL) oil and 1/4 tsp (1 mL) each salt and pepper; toss well. Spread eggplant out evenly; bake, stirring once, for 20 minutes or until tender and golden brown. Remove from oven; set aside.

3. Line a sieve with paper towels; drain porcini mushrooms through sieve, reserving soaking liquid. Rinse porcini mushrooms under running water; pat dry on paper towels. Chop coarsely.

4. In a large pot of boiling salted water, cook penne for 8 to 10 minutes or until tender but firm.

5. Meanwhile, in a large skillet, heat remaining oil over medium heat. Add porcini mushrooms, fresh mushrooms, prosciutto, garlic and rosemary; cook, stirring, for 3 to 5 minutes or until fresh mushrooms are tender. Add eggplant; stir well.

6. Drain pasta in a colander but do not rinse. Return pasta to pot over low heat. Add eggplant mixture, ricotta cheese and enough of the reserved porcini soaking liquid to make a creamy sauce. Add remaining salt and pepper; toss to combine well. If desired, season to taste with additional salt and pepper. Serve at once in warm pasta bowls, garnished with fresh rosemary.

Shrimp pasta with lemon-tarragon sauce

Serves 4 to 6

My good friend, food writer Rose Murray, came up with an easy way to cook the vegetables for this pasta sauce. Place the broccoli, carrot and green onions in a colander. When the pasta is ready, drain through the colander; the hot water will cook the vegetables.

2 cups	tiny broccoli florets and thinly sliced stems	500 mL
1	large carrot, peeled and shredded	1
4	green onions, cut diagonally into 1/2-inch (1 cm) pieces	4
4 cups	small pasta shells	1 L
1	bay leaf	1
1 tbsp	butter	15 mL
1 tbsp	canola oil or vegetable oil	15 mL
1 lb	raw large shrimp, peeled, deveined and patted dry	500 g
1	clove garlic, minced	1
1/2 cup	chicken stock	125 mL
2 tbsp	fresh lemon juice	25 mL
1 tsp	minced fresh tarragon (or 1/2 tsp/2 mL dried)	5 mL
1/4 tsp	black pepper	1 mL
Pinch	salt	Pinch
Pinch	cayenne pepper	Pinch
1/2 cup	sour cream	125 mL
1 tbsp	Dijon mustard	15 mL
	Chopped fresh parsley	

1. In a colander, combine broccoli, carrot and green onions; set aside. In a large pot of boiling salted water, cook pasta with bay leaf for 8 to 10 minutes or until tender but firm.

2. While pasta is cooking, in a large heavy skillet, heat butter and oil over medium-high heat. Add shrimp and garlic; cook for 2 to 3 minutes or until shrimp are pink. With a slotted spoon, transfer shrimp and garlic to a plate; set aside and keep warm.

3. Return skillet, with any remaining juices, to heat. Add chicken stock, lemon juice, tarragon, pepper, salt and cayenne pepper. Bring to a boil over medium-high heat, scraping up any brown bits from bottom of skillet. Boil for 2 to 3 minutes or until liquid is reduced by about half.

4. When pasta is ready, drain through colander containing vegetables. Discard bay leaf. Return pasta and vegetables to pot over low heat; gently stir in shrimp and garlic. Add sour cream and mustard to mixture in skillet; stir well. Pour sauce over pasta, stirring gently. Serve at once in warm pasta bowls, garnished with chopped parsley.

Quick tomato pizza

Serves 6 to 8

*This almost instant
pizza uses Italian-style
flatbread topped with
sliced tomatoes, feta
cheese and pesto. For a
Mediterranean-themed
meal, serve with
Mushroom and
Prosciutto Antipasto
with Walnuts (see
recipe, page 33) or
Lentil and Pancetta
Antipasto (see recipe,
page 36).*

Kitchen Wisdom

Pesto is a vibrant Italian
condiment made of basil,
olive oil and garlic. Look
for it in the sauce section
of your supermarket.

• Baking sheet

1	12-inch (30 cm) Italian-style flatbread	1
⅓ cup	pesto	75 mL
3	medium tomatoes, thinly sliced	3
¼ tsp	salt	1 mL
¼ tsp	black pepper	1 mL
1 cup	crumbled feta cheese (about 5 oz/150 g)	250 mL

1. Preheat oven to 425°F (220°C). Place flatbread on baking sheet; spread evenly with pesto. Arrange tomato slices in overlapping circles on top of pesto; sprinkle with salt and pepper then feta cheese. Bake for 10 to 12 minutes or until feta starts to brown. Cut into wedges; serve at once.

Make Ahead
The flatbread can be topped with the ingredients and then refrigerated, covered, for up to 2 hours before baking.

Jalapeño-cheese corn bread

Makes 12 pieces

The cheese provides richness while the jalapeño peppers add a subtle kick to this easy bread.

• 9-inch (2.5 L) square baking pan, greased

1 cup	all-purpose flour	250 mL
1 cup	cornmeal	250 mL
1 cup	shredded Monterey Jack or mozzarella cheese (about 4 oz/125 g)	250 mL
1 tbsp	finely chopped drained, pickled jalapeño peppers	15 mL
1 tbsp	baking powder	15 mL
1 tbsp	granulated sugar	15 mL
1/2 tsp	salt	2 mL
1 cup	milk	250 mL
1	egg	1
2 tbsp	butter, melted	25 mL

1. Preheat oven to 400°F (200°C). In a large bowl, stir together flour, cornmeal, cheese, jalapeño peppers, baking powder, sugar and salt. In a 2-cup (500 mL) liquid measure, whisk together milk, egg and butter until well combined. Add to flour mixture all at once; mix just until no dry spots remain.

2. Spoon batter into pan, spreading evenly. Bake for 18 to 20 minutes or until bread is light golden, well risen and pulling away from sides of pan. Let cool in pan on wire rack for 5 minutes. Cut into 12 pieces and serve warm.

> **Make Ahead**
> Baked bread can be frozen for up to 1 month. Thaw the bread, wrap in foil and reheat at 350°F (180°C) for 20 minutes.

Cranberry-cornmeal muffins

Makes 12 muffins

These pretty muffins, with their slight crunch of cornmeal, are not too sweet and make a great substitute for dinner rolls at Thanksgiving or Christmas.

You can use fresh, frozen or dried cranberries here; if using frozen berries, bake the muffins 3 to 5 minutes longer.

To make a sweeter, breakfast-type muffin, increase the amount of sugar to $1/3$ cup (75 mL).

Kitchen Wisdom

Here is a quick and clean way to grease muffin pans: Give each cup a quick squirt of baking spray then wipe with a pastry brush or paper towel.

• 12-cup muffin pan, lightly greased or lined with paper baking cups

1 $1/2$ cups	all-purpose flour	375 mL
$1/2$ cup	cornmeal	125 mL
$1/4$ cup	granulated sugar	50 mL
2 tsp	baking powder	10 mL
1 tsp	baking soda	5 mL
$1/2$ tsp	salt	2 mL
1 cup	plain yogurt	250 mL
$1/4$ cup	vegetable oil	50 mL
$1/4$ cup	orange juice	50 mL
1	egg	1
1 cup	cranberries	250 mL

1. Preheat oven to 375°F (190°C). In a large bowl, stir together flour, cornmeal, sugar, baking powder, baking soda and salt.

2. In a 2-cup (500 mL) liquid measure, whisk together yogurt, oil, orange juice and egg until smooth. Add yogurt mixture to flour mixture all at once; mix just until no dry spots remain. Stir in cranberries.

3. Spoon batter into prepared muffin pan, dividing evenly among cups. Bake for 15 to 18 minutes or until firm and a toothpick inserted into center muffin comes out clean. Let cool in pan on wire rack for 5 minutes. Remove muffins from pan; cool on wire rack.

> ### Make Ahead
> These muffins are best served the day they're baked, but can be frozen for up to 1 month immediately after cooling. Thaw the muffins then warm in microwave on High for 30 seconds per muffin or in a 300°F (150°C) oven for 10 to 15 minutes before serving.

Herbaceous Soup (page 41)
Overleaf: Mediterranean Vegetables with Roasted-Garlic Couscous (page 76)

Spiced pear biscuits

Makes 8 biscuits

These wedge-shaped biscuits get their subtle spicing from Chinese five-spice powder, a blend of cinnamon, cloves, fennel seeds, star anise and Szechuan peppercorns.

For another recipe using five-spice powder, try Savoy Cabbage Sauté (see recipe, page 131).

For an easy alternative to dessert, serve these biscuits warm with grapes and a selection of cheeses.

Kitchen Wisdom

Look for Chinese five-spice powder in bulk stores or the Asian section of most large supermarkets.

• 9-inch (1.5 L) round cake pan, lightly greased

2½ cups	all-purpose flour	625 mL
¼ cup	granulated sugar	50 mL
4 tsp	baking powder	20 mL
1 tsp	salt	5 mL
½ tsp	Chinese five-spice powder	2 mL
⅓ cup	shortening	75 mL
1 cup	finely chopped peeled, cored pears	250 mL
2 tbsp	fresh lemon juice	25 mL
	Milk	

1. Preheat oven to 425°F (220°C). In a large bowl, stir together flour, sugar, baking powder, salt and five-spice powder. With a pastry blender or two knives, cut in shortening until mixture resembles coarse bread crumbs. Stir in pears.

2. Pour lemon juice into a 1-cup (250 mL) liquid measure; add enough milk to yield 1 cup (250 mL). Add milk mixture to flour mixture all at once; stir just until the dry ingredients are moistened. The dough will be quite moist.

3. Transfer dough to prepared pan, spreading evenly with a spatula to fill pan. Bake for 35 to 40 minutes or until well risen and golden. Turn biscuit out on wire rack; cool slightly. Cut into wedges; serve warm.

> ## Make Ahead
> These biscuits are best served the day they're baked, but can be frozen for up to 1 month immediately after cooling. Thaw biscuits then warm in microwave on High for 30 seconds per biscuit, or in a 300°F (150°C) oven for 10 to 15 minutes before serving.

Herbed soda bread

Makes 12 slices

This fragrant, quickly made bread is best served freshly baked. If necessary, however, it can be baked, cooled, frozen then reheated at a later date.

• Baking sheet, lightly greased

3 cups	all-purpose flour	750 mL
3 tbsp	chopped fresh parsley	45 mL
1½ tsp	dried thyme	7 mL
1½ tsp	crumbled dried rosemary	7 mL
1 tsp	baking powder	5 mL
1 tsp	baking soda	5 mL
1 tsp	salt	5 mL
2 tbsp	fresh lemon juice	25 mL
	Milk	
¼ cup	butter, melted	50 mL

1. Preheat oven to 375°F (190°C). In a large bowl, stir together flour, parsley, thyme, rosemary, baking powder, baking soda and salt.

2. Pour lemon juice into a 1-cup (250 mL) liquid measure; add enough milk to yield 1 cup (250 mL). Stir butter into milk mixture. First with a fork, then with your hands, work milk into flour until dough holds together.

3. Turn dough out onto lightly floured work surface; knead lightly for 2 minutes or until a smooth dough forms. Pat dough into a 1½-inch (4 cm) thick disk; place on baking sheet. With a sharp knife, make a cross ½ inch (1 cm) deep in top of dough; sprinkle lightly with flour. Bake for 45 to 50 minutes or until loaf is golden and sounds hollow when tapped on its base. Let cool on a wire rack for 10 minutes. Cut into slices; serve warm, spread with butter.

> **Make Ahead**
> Baked bread can be frozen for up to 1 month. Thaw the bread, wrap in foil and reheat in a 350°F (180°C) oven for 20 minutes.

Fish, seafood and vegetarian

See also...

Molasses-glazed salmon on mesclun

Serves 6

This light but rich-tasting main course features beautifully glazed salmon atop crisp greens with a warm sweet-sour dressing.

Kitchen Wisdom

Mesclun is a trendy mix of different salad leaves, available in bulk in the produce section of most large supermarkets. It's a convenient way to make a salad in a hurry as it needs only the briefest rinsing then a quick spin in the salad spinner.

If you don't have a 12-inch (30 cm) ovenproof skillet, use a smaller one and cook salmon in batches. To make skillet handle ovenproof, cover with a double layer of foil.

Make Ahead
Salmon must be marinated in the refrigerator for up to 2 hours.

- Shallow baking dish
- 12-inch (30 cm) ovenproof skillet

Salmon

1/3 cup	olive oil	75 mL
1/4 cup	molasses	50 mL
2	cloves garlic, minced	2
6	salmon fillets with skin, each about 6 oz (175 g)	6

Salad

9 cups	mesclun or other salad greens, washed and dried, larger leaves torn into pieces	2.25 L
1/4 cup	cider vinegar or white wine vinegar	50 mL
1/4 tsp	salt	1 mL
1/4 tsp	black pepper	1 mL

1. **Salmon:** In the baking dish, whisk together 1/4 cup (50 mL) olive oil, molasses and garlic. Add salmon, turning to coat on all sides. Refrigerate, covered, for 2 hours, turning salmon occasionally.

2. Preheat broiler. Remove salmon from marinade, shaking off excess; reserve marinade. In the skillet, heat remaining oil over medium-high heat. Add salmon to skillet, skin-side down; cook for 2 to 3 minutes. Turn salmon; cook for 2 to 3 minutes or until flesh is just opaque and flakes easily with a fork (salmon should still be slightly coral-colored in center). Place skillet under preheated broiler. Broil for 1 to 2 minutes or until skin is crisp and golden.

3. **Salad:** Divide greens among 6 dinner plates. Return skillet, with oil remaining in it, to burner; add reserved marinade, vinegar, salt and pepper. Bring to a boil over medium-high heat, stirring to scrape up any browned bits from bottom of skillet. Place 1 salmon fillet on each portion of greens; drizzle fish and greens with hot dressing. Serve at once.

Greek swordfish with tomatoes and feta

Serves 6

Some years ago, Cheryl Embrett, a colleague of mine when I worked at Homemaker's Magazine, visited Greece and came back with a fabulous recipe for shrimp baked with tomatoes and topped with feta. It became a firm favorite on the magazine's dinner-party circuit. Here's my version of the recipe, using meaty swordfish steaks, which stay beautifully moist when cooked this way.

Kitchen Wisdom

If swordfish is unavailable, substitute halibut, tuna or marlin steaks.

Make Ahead
Tomato sauce can be refrigerated, covered, for up to 3 days. Reheat until piping hot before pouring over swordfish steaks.

• 13- by 9-inch (3 L) baking dish, lightly oiled

2 tbsp	olive oil	25 mL
1	large onion, halved and thinly sliced	1
2	cloves garlic, minced	2
1	can (28 oz/796 mL) diced tomatoes	1
1/3 cup	chopped fresh basil or oregano (or 2 tsp/10 mL dried)	75 mL
1/4 cup	dry white wine or orange juice	50 mL
2 tbsp	tomato paste	25 mL
1 tsp	liquid honey	5 mL
1/4 tsp	salt	1 mL
1/4 tsp	black pepper	1 mL
1	bay leaf	1
6	swordfish steaks, each about 6 oz (175 g)	6
1 cup	crumbled feta cheese (about 5 oz/150 g)	250 mL
	Fresh basil, oregano or parsley	

1. Preheat oven to 400°F (200°C). In a large skillet, heat oil over medium-high heat. Add onion and garlic; cook, stirring, for 3 to 5 minutes or until onion is soft but not brown.

2. Stir in tomatoes, basil, wine, tomato paste, honey, salt, pepper and bay leaf. Increase heat to high; bring to a boil. Reduce heat to medium; simmer, uncovered and stirring occasionally, for 8 to 10 minutes or until sauce has thickened slightly. Discard bay leaf.

3. In the baking dish, arrange swordfish steaks in a single layer; cover with tomato mixture. Bake, uncovered, for 10 to 15 minutes or until sauce is bubbly; sprinkle with feta cheese. Bake for another 5 to 10 minutes or until steaks are opaque, flake easily with a fork, and feta is starting to brown. Serve garnished with basil.

Thai fish parcels

The posh way to describe this method of cooking is en papillote, *meaning literally (if not so exotically) "in a package." The parchment or foil parcels seal in all the lovely juices and seasonings, making this a flavorful — and low-fat — way to cook fish. Once the fish is cooked, slit the parcels open and empty the contents over Asian noodles or rice.*

Any type of fish fillets can be used in this recipe — salmon, orange roughy, cod or red snapper, for instance.

Make Ahead

If using parchment, fish and flavorings can be wrapped and refrigerated for up to 8 hours before cooking. If using foil, cook fish as soon as it's wrapped to prevent the acid in the lemon juice from reacting with the aluminum foil.

- Six 15- by 10-inch (37.5 by 25 cm) rectangles of parchment paper or aluminum foil, lightly oiled
- Baking sheet

6	fish fillets (each 6 oz/175 g), thawed if frozen	6
1½ cups	sliced shiitake mushrooms, stems removed (about 6 oz/ 175 g with stems)	375 mL
1 tbsp	minced ginger root	15 mL
2	cloves garlic, minced	2
½ tsp	salt	2 mL
½ tsp	black pepper	2 mL
2 tbsp	sesame oil	25 mL
	Hot pepper sauce to taste	
⅓ cup	chopped fresh coriander	75 mL
12	large fresh basil leaves	12
1	small lemon, cut into 6 slices	1
2 tbsp	finely chopped green onion	25 mL

1. Preheat oven to 450°F (230°C). Place 1 fish fillet on one half of each piece of parchment. Top fish with shiitake mushrooms, dividing evenly. Sprinkle with ginger, garlic, salt and pepper. Drizzle with sesame oil; add a dash of hot pepper sauce. Sprinkle with coriander; top each with 2 basil leaves and 1 lemon slice.

2. Fold parchment in half to enclose ingredients. Starting at a corner near fold, turn in edges all around, pleating and pinching to seal well. Place packages on baking sheet. Bake for 10 to 12 minutes or until fish is opaque and flakes easily with a fork.

3. Open packages carefully, avoiding steam. Discard basil and lemon slices. Spoon fish and cooking juices onto dinner plates. Garnish with green onion; serve at once.

Sole fillets stuffed with prosciutto

Serves 6

This elegant treatment of sole can be prepared ahead of time and then baked just before serving. Team with sautéed potatoes and a green vegetable, such as Herb-Glazed Brussels Sprouts (see recipe, page 130).

Make Ahead
Sole fillets can be stuffed then refrigerated, covered, for up to 8 hours.

- 12 wooden toothpicks
- 11- by 7-inch (2 L) baking dish, lightly greased

12	large sole fillets (each about 3 oz/ 75 g), thawed if frozen	12
6 oz	prosciutto, trimmed of excess fat and finely minced	175 g
12	large fresh basil leaves, slivered	12
1/4 tsp	black pepper	1 mL
3/4 cup	dry white wine	175 mL
3 tbsp	dry bread crumbs	45 mL
3 tbsp	freshly grated Parmesan cheese	45 mL
1/3 cup	whipping (35%) cream	75 mL
	Fresh basil sprigs	

1. Preheat oven to 375°F (190°C). Lay sole fillets on work surface. Divide prosciutto evenly among fillets. Sprinkle lightly with basil and pepper. Starting from narrow end, roll up each fillet to enclose prosciutto and basil; secure with toothpick. Arrange sole fillets seam-side down in baking dish. Pour wine around fillets.

2. In a small bowl, stir together bread crumbs and Parmesan cheese; sprinkle evenly over fillets. Bake, uncovered, for 20 to 25 minutes or until sole is opaque and flakes easily with a fork.

3. With a slotted spoon, remove sole fillets from dish; keep warm. Pour cooking juices from baking dish into a small saucepan; stir in cream. Bring to a boil over high heat; boil, stirring occasionally, for 2 minutes or until sauce has reduced and thickened slightly (sauce will not be very thick).

4. Remove toothpick from each fillet. Divide fillets among 6 warm dinner plates; drizzle sauce around each portion. Serve garnished with basil sprigs.

Seafood pie with rösti topping

Serves 6

Don't let the lengthy list of ingredients put you off trying this easy seafood pie. With its creamy sauce and crisp potato topping, it's a comforting main dish to serve on a wintry day.

If you thought smooth sauces only come in packages, try the simple method used in this recipe. You're guaranteed a lump-free sauce every time.

To make the pie a little bit special, look for interesting mixtures of frozen vegetables, such as the Mediterranean mixes available in some supermarkets.

- 11- by 7-inch (2 L) baking dish
- Foil-lined baking sheet

Filling

1 1/4 cups	cold milk	300 mL
1 cup	dry white wine	250 mL
1/3 cup	all-purpose flour	75 mL
1/4 cup	butter, cubed	50 mL
1 lb	cod or haddock fillets, cut into 1-inch (2.5 cm) pieces	500 g
8 oz	raw large shrimp, peeled and deveined	250 g
8 oz	scallops	250 g
2 cups	frozen mixed vegetables	500 mL
4 oz	smoked salmon, coarsely chopped	125 g
1/2 cup	chopped green onions	125 mL
1/4 cup	chopped fresh parsley	50 mL
1/4 cup	drained, minced dill pickles	50 mL
2 tbsp	chopped fresh dill (or 1 tsp/5 mL dried)	25 mL
1 tsp	Worcestershire sauce	5 mL
1/2 tsp	black pepper	2 mL
1/4 tsp	salt	1 mL
1	bay leaf	1

Topping

1 lb	Yukon Gold potatoes, peeled	500 g
2 tbsp	butter, melted	25 mL
1/4 tsp	salt	1 mL
1/4 tsp	black pepper	1 mL

About 2 large potatoes equals 1 lb (500 g).

1. **Filling:** In a large saucepan over medium-high heat, combine milk, wine and flour; whisk until smooth. Stir in butter. Bring to a boil, whisking constantly, until butter melts and mixture is smooth and bubbly. Reduce heat to medium; cook, whisking constantly, for 2 minutes or until smooth.

2. Add fish, shrimp, scallops, vegetables, smoked salmon, green onions, parsley, dill pickles, dill, Worcestershire sauce, pepper, salt and bay leaf; stir gently. Spoon into baking dish; set aside.

3. **Topping:** In a large saucepan over high heat, combine potatoes and just enough cold water to cover them; bring to a boil. Reduce heat to medium-low; cook, covered, for 15 to 20 minutes or until potatoes are almost tender. Drain well; set aside until cool enough to handle.

4. Preheat oven to 400°F (200°C). Using the largest holes of a cheese grater, grate potatoes into a medium bowl. Add butter, salt and pepper; mix with a fork until well combined. Immediately spoon potato mixture evenly over fish mixture to cover completely.

5. Bake for 40 to 45 minutes or until filling is bubbly and potato topping starts to brown. If necessary, heat broiler and broil for 2 to 3 minutes or until topping is golden. Discard bay leaf at serving time.

> **Make Ahead**
> The filling can be spooned into an 11- by 7-inch (2 L) baking dish, then refrigerated, covered, for up to 8 hours.

Light Asian fondue

Serves 4 to 6

Fondues are the answer to every lazy host's prayers. After all, what could be better than having your guests cook their own meal? This low-fat version uses broth instead of oil to cook morsels of seafood then, at the end of dinner, as is the Asian custom, spinach and noodles are added to transform the flavorful broth into a hearty soup.

If you prefer, substitute boneless skinless chicken breasts (trimmed of excess fat and cut into 1-inch/ 2.5 cm pieces) for some or all of the seafood.

• Fondue pot and fondue forks

Asian Dipping Sauce

¼ cup	balsamic vinegar	50 mL
¼ cup	soya sauce	50 mL
2 tbsp	packed brown sugar	25 mL
2 tsp	minced ginger root	10 mL
1	clove garlic, minced	1
¼ cup	chopped green onions	50 mL

Fondue

1 lb	scallops	500 g
1 lb	raw large shrimp, peeled and deveined	500 g
	Fresh coriander sprigs	
2 cups	shredded spinach, tough stems discarded	500 mL
1 cup	egg noodles	250 mL
4 cups	chicken stock	1 L
¼ cup	chopped green onions	50 mL
2 tbsp	coarsely chopped fresh coriander	25 mL
3	¼-inch (5 mm) slices ginger root	3
1	clove garlic, sliced	1
1	2-inch (5 cm) strip lemon zest	1

1. **Asian Dipping Sauce:** In a small bowl, combine balsamic vinegar, soya sauce, brown sugar, ginger and garlic; stir to blend well. Let stand at room temperature for 2 hours. Just before serving, strain through a fine sieve into a ¾-cup (175 mL) serving bowl; stir in green onions.

2. **Fondue:** Arrange scallops and shrimp on a large serving platter; garnish with coriander sprigs. Place spinach and noodles in separate serving bowls; set aside.

3. In the fondue pot set on stovetop, combine chicken stock, onions, coriander, ginger, garlic and lemon zest; bring to a boil. Reduce heat to medium; simmer for 5 minutes. Transfer pot to fondue burner; light burner.

4. To serve, spear seafood on fondue forks. Cook in simmering broth for 3 to 5 minutes or until scallops and shrimp are opaque. Dip in sauce before eating.

5. When seafood is finished, add spinach and noodles to broth in fondue pot; cook for 3 to 5 minutes or until spinach is wilted and noodles are just tender. Ladle broth, spinach and noodles into soup bowls, discarding ginger, garlic and lemon zest. Serve at once.

Make Ahead

Scallops and shrimp can be arranged on a serving platter and then refrigerated, tightly covered, for up to 8 hours.

Allow the dipping sauce to stand at room temperature for at least 2 hours before serving for flavors to blend.

Mediterranean vegetables with roasted-garlic couscous

Serves 4 to 6

Roasting vegetables seems to intensify their flavors. Here they're served atop garlicky couscous which transforms them into a vegetarian main dish that will please even the most confirmed carnivore. It is fast to fix and the gorgeous aroma of roasting vegetables wafting from your oven will transport you to southern Europe.

• Large shallow roasting pan

3	large plum tomatoes, each cut in half lengthwise	3
2	small green zucchini, halved lengthwise and cut diagonally into 1-inch (2.5 cm) slices	2
2	small yellow zucchini, halved lengthwise and cut diagonally into 1-inch (2.5 cm) slices	2
1	red bell pepper, seeded and cut into 1-inch (2.5 cm) pieces	1
1	green bell pepper, seeded and cut into 1-inch (2.5 cm) pieces	1
1	large red onion, cut into 6 wedges	1
8	large cloves garlic, unpeeled	8
2	bay leaves	2
1	10-inch (25 cm) sprig fresh rosemary, cut in half	1
1/2 tsp	salt	2 mL
1/2 tsp	black pepper	2 mL
1/4 cup	olive oil	50 mL
1	package (12 oz/375 g) couscous (2 cups/500 mL)	1
	Chicken stock	
1 cup	crumbled feta cheese (about 5 oz/150 g)	250 mL
	Fresh rosemary sprigs	

1. Preheat oven to 400°F (200°C). In the roasting pan, combine tomatoes, green zucchini, yellow zucchini, red pepper, green pepper, onion, garlic, 1 bay leaf, rosemary, salt and pepper. Drizzle with 2 tbsp (25 mL) olive oil; toss to coat well. Roast, uncovered, stirring occasionally, for 40 to 50 minutes or until vegetables are tender and just starting to brown. Remove garlic; set aside. Keep remaining vegetables warm.

2. Prepare couscous according to package directions, using chicken stock instead of water, omitting any butter and adding remaining bay leaf to stock.

3. Squeeze garlic cloves out of skins. In a small bowl, mash garlic with a fork until fairly smooth. Whisk in remaining oil until well combined.

4. When couscous is cooked, fluff with a fork. Add garlic mixture; stir until well combined. Spoon couscous into warm shallow serving dish; discard bay leaf. Spoon vegetables over couscous; discard rosemary and bay leaf. Serve sprinkled with feta cheese and garnished with rosemary. (Alternatively, let your guests add feta cheese at the table.)

Watercress and feta tart with olive pastry

Serves 6

Olive oil makes the pastry for this tart crisp and wonderfully flavorful. The pastry is prepared in the food processor, is easy to work with and doesn't need weighting with baking beans during baking.

For best results, serve tart warm or at room temperature.

For an impressive sit-down appetizer, simply cut the tart into slimmer wedges.

- 9- or 10-inch (22.5 or 25 cm) tart pan with a removable base
- Baking sheet

Pastry

1½ cups	all-purpose flour	375 mL
¼ tsp	salt	1 mL
⅓ cup	olive oil	75 mL
2 tbsp	fresh lemon juice	25 mL
2 tbsp	cold water	25 mL

Filling

1 tbsp	olive oil	15 mL
½ cup	finely chopped red onion	125 mL
3 cups	chopped watercress, washed and dried, tough stems discarded	750 mL
1 cup	crumbled feta cheese (about 5 oz/150 g)	250 mL
1	can (5 oz/160 mL) evaporated milk	1
2	eggs, beaten	2
1 tsp	grated lemon zest	5 mL
¼ tsp	black pepper	1 mL
¼ tsp	freshly grated nutmeg	1 mL
	Mixed salad greens or watercress	

1. **Pastry:** Preheat oven to 375°F (190°C). In a food processor, combine flour and salt; process briefly to mix. With motor running, add olive oil, lemon juice and water; process until crumbly. Turn mixture into tart pan and, with your fingertips, press dough evenly over base and up sides of pan. Bake for 10 minutes or until pastry is crisp. Don't worry if the base cracks slightly. Set aside, leaving oven on.

2. Filling: In a large skillet, heat oil over medium-high heat. Add red onion and cook, stirring, for 2 to 3 minutes or until soft but not brown. Add watercress and cook, stirring, for 1 to 2 minutes just until watercress wilts. Remove from heat. Spoon into a bowl; set aside to cool slightly.

3. Add cheese, milk, eggs, lemon zest, pepper and nutmeg to watercress; stir well. Spoon into tart shell, spreading evenly. Bake for 20 minutes or until filling is just set in center. Serve warm or at room temperature, garnished with mixed salad greens or watercress.

Make Ahead

The pastry can be refrigerated, tightly wrapped, for up to 3 days. Let stand at room temperature for at least 30 minutes before pressing into tart pan.

The baked tart can be refrigerated, covered, for up to 24 hours. Let stand at room temperature for 30 minutes before serving.

Sautéed portobellos with rapini and roasted peppers

Serves 6

One of my favorite Toronto chefs is Chris McDonald, owner of Cava restaurant. At his previous restaurant, Avalon, Chris served this layered vegetarian dish as an appetizer, but I've increased the quantities to make a splendid meatless main course. (If you'd rather serve it as an appetizer, simply halve all the ingredients, except the oil.)

Chris prepares his own baba gannoujh and roasted red peppers from scratch, of course, but the ready-made versions available in most supermarkets make good — and speedy — substitutes.

Kitchen Wisdom

Reserve the mushroom stems for use in stock or soup.

Rapini is a leafy green vegetable that looks like skinny broccoli and is sometimes called broccoli rabe. To prepare it, simply trim off the stalk ends.

2	bunches rapini (about 2 lbs/1 kg)	2
6	large slices sourdough bread, about ½ inch (1 cm) thick	6
¾ cup	baba gannoujh	175 mL
2 tbsp	olive oil	25 mL
12	3-inch (7.5 cm) portobello mushroom caps, wiped clean with damp paper towels	12
½ tsp	salt	2 mL
½ tsp	black pepper	2 mL
2	cloves garlic, minced	2
2 cups	drained bottled roasted red peppers	500 mL
1½ cups	coarsely shredded Romano or Parmesan cheese (about 5 oz/150 g)	375 mL

1. Preheat broiler to high. In a large saucepan of boiling salted water, cook rapini for 1 minute. Drain well; set aside.

2. Meanwhile, with a 3-inch (7.5 cm) pastry cutter or the top of a 3-inch (7.5 cm) water glass, cut out 2 rounds from each slice of bread. Place rounds under broiler; toast on both sides until lightly golden. Spread each piece of toast with 1 tbsp (15 mL) baba gannoujh; set aside.

3. In a large heavy skillet, heat 1 tbsp (15 mL) oil over medium-high heat. Add mushroom caps; cook, turning once and sprinkling with ¼ tsp (1 mL) each salt and pepper, for 4 to 6 minutes or until golden and tender. Remove from skillet; keep warm.

Baba gannoujh (pronounced "baba ganoosh") is a flavorful roasted eggplant dip of middle-eastern origin. Look for it in the deli section of your supermarket.

Roasted red peppers are available in jars in the pickle section of your supermarket.

4. Add remaining oil to skillet and heat over medium-high heat. Add rapini, garlic and remaining salt and pepper. Cook, stirring, for 1 to 2 minutes or until rapini and garlic are tender but garlic is not browned. In a microwaveable bowl, microwave red peppers on High for 1 to 2 minutes or until piping hot.

5. Divide rapini among 6 plates, mounding in the center of each plate. Top each mound with 2 slices of toast, side by side, with baba gannoujh facing up. Divide roasted red peppers evenly among toast; sprinkle with cheese. Top each serving with 2 mushroom caps. Serve at once.

Onion tarte tatin

Serves 6

Traditional tarte tatin is an upside-down apple tart with a caramel topping. So it occurred to me that what works well for apples should be equally good for onions, since slow-cooking makes them delectably sweet. The result? A perfect vegetarian tarte tatin.

Serve with Escarole Salad with Olives (see recipe, page 146), sprinkled with crumbled feta cheese, or with green beans tossed with olive oil, lemon juice and some chopped fresh herbs. The tarte tatin also makes a fine accompaniment to a main course.

Kitchen Wisdom

Choose sweet Vidalia, Spanish or Bermuda onions for this recipe.

To speed up preparation of the onions, use a food processor fitted with a slicing disk.

Capers are the pickled flower buds of a bush that grows in the Mediterranean region. They have a distinctive, pleasantly astringent flavor. Look for them in the pickle section of your supermarket.

- 9-inch (22.5 cm) pie plate, lightly buttered
- Baking sheet

2 tbsp	butter	25 mL
2	large sweet onions, thinly sliced	2
½ tsp	salt	2 mL
½ tsp	black pepper	2 mL
2 tbsp	balsamic vinegar	25 mL
½ tsp	dried thyme	2 mL
2 tbsp	drained capers	25 mL
1	package (14 oz/397 g) frozen puff pastry (2 pieces), thawed	1

1. In a large heavy saucepan or Dutch oven, melt butter over medium-high heat. Add onions, salt and pepper; stir to coat well. Reduce heat to low; cook, covered, for 15 minutes. Add vinegar and thyme. Cook, covered and stirring occasionally, for 30 to 40 minutes or until onions are very tender. Remove from heat; stir in capers. Let cool slightly. Spoon into pie plate; set aside.

2. Preheat oven to 425°F (220°C). On a lightly floured surface, roll out each piece of pastry to a 10- by 6-inch (25 by 15 cm) rectangle. Dampen 1 long edge of each piece. Join pastry edges together to make a 10-inch (25 cm) square, overlapping edges by about ½ inch (1 cm); press to seal well. Cover onion mixture with pastry; press around edges with a fork to seal. Trim any overhanging pastry; make slits in pastry for steam to escape. Transfer pie to baking sheet. Bake for 25 minutes or until pastry is puffed and golden.

3. Run a knife under edge of pastry to loosen from pie plate. Place a cutting board or large platter over pie dish. Invert pie dish and cutting board so that tarte tatin falls, pastry-side down, onto board. Cut into wedges; serve hot.

> **Make Ahead**
> Onions can be cooked then refrigerated, covered, for up to 2 days.

Poultry

See also...

The ultimate roast chicken

Serves 6

Golden roast chicken flecked with herbs is one of my favorite main dishes — and it's so easy to do.

Ever wonder what to do with the packet of giblets that comes with your roasting chicken? Many people just throw them out. My mother used to boil up giblets for the cat's dinner. But I think this recipe is a far better use for them. The sun-dried tomatoes and porcini mushrooms add wonderful depth of flavor to the stock, but you can omit them if you like.

If your chicken doesn't come with giblets, use 2 cups (500 mL) chicken stock (or a mixture of stock and white wine) to make the gravy.

• Shallow roasting pan with oiled rack

Chicken

1	air-chilled roasting chicken (about $3\frac{1}{2}$ lbs/1.75 kg), giblets and neck removed for stock (below)	1
3	cloves garlic, unpeeled, crushed with flat blade of large knife	3
$\frac{1}{3}$ cup	fresh parsley sprigs	75 mL
$\frac{1}{3}$ cup	fresh thyme sprigs	75 mL
1	small lemon, cut in half	1
1 tbsp	olive oil	15 mL
1 tsp	fresh thyme leaves	5 mL
$\frac{1}{4}$ tsp	salt	1 mL
$\frac{1}{4}$ tsp	pepper	1 mL
	Fresh thyme or parsley sprigs	

Giblet Stock

3 cups	water	750 mL
	Chicken giblets and neck	
1	small onion, unpeeled, cut into quarters	1
2	sun-dried tomatoes	2
1 tbsp	dried porcini mushrooms	15 mL
1 tsp	whole black peppercorns	5 mL
$\frac{1}{2}$ tsp	salt	2 mL
1	bay leaf	1

Gravy

2 tbsp	cornstarch	25 mL
2 tbsp	cold water	25 mL

Kitchen Wisdom

For best flavor, buy an air-chilled chicken (check on the label or ask your butcher) and use fresh rather than dried herbs. This recipe calls for parsley and thyme, but use whatever is available in your herb garden or local store. Tarragon, oregano, marjoram, sage or basil are all good choices.

Make Ahead
Stock can be refrigerated, covered, for up to 3 days or frozen for up to 3 months.

1. **Chicken:** Preheat oven to 450°F (230°C). Snip off any string from chicken. Pull out any visible excess fat from cavity of chicken. Tuck wing tips under chicken. Place chicken on rack in roasting pan.

2. Put garlic, parsley and thyme sprigs in cavity of chicken. Squeeze lemon evenly over chicken. Add lemon halves to cavity. Drizzle olive oil over chicken; rub into breasts, legs and wings with palms of your hands. Sprinkle with thyme leaves, salt and pepper.

3. Roast chicken, uncovered, for 30 minutes. Reduce oven temperature to 375°F (190°C); cook for 45 to 60 minutes or until a meat thermometer inserted into thickest part of thigh registers 185°F (85°C) and juices that run out of thigh are no longer pink. Transfer chicken to a warm platter. Let stand, loosely covered with foil, for 10 minutes. Remove rack from roasting pan; pour cooking juices into a small bowl. Place bowl in freezer.

4. **Giblet stock:** While chicken is roasting, in a medium saucepan over high heat, combine water, giblets and neck, onion, sun-dried tomatoes, mushrooms, peppercorns, salt and bay leaf; bring to a boil. Reduce heat to low; simmer gently, partially covered, for 1 hour. Remove from heat; strain through a fine sieve into a medium bowl.

5. **Gravy:** In a small bowl, combine cornstarch and water; stir until smooth. Pour giblet stock into roasting pan. Bring to a boil over high heat, stirring to scrape up any browned bits from bottom of pan. Whisk cornstarch mixture into gravy; bring to a boil, whisking constantly. Reduce heat to medium-low; simmer, whisking occasionally, for 3 to 5 minutes or until gravy is thickened and smooth.

6. Remove cooking juices from freezer; carefully skim and discard fat that has risen to top. Add juices to gravy, along with juices accumulated under chicken. If desired, season to taste with additional salt and pepper. Pour gravy into a pitcher. Garnish chicken with thyme and serve with gravy.

Braised chicken and apples with grainy mustard sauce

Serves 4 to 6

Serve this simple casserole with mashed potatoes or rice and a crisp green vegetable, such as Savoy Cabbage Sauté (see recipe, page 131).

• Wide shallow flameproof casserole or Dutch oven

1 tbsp	olive oil	15 mL
1 tbsp	butter	15 mL
4 lbs	chicken thighs and drumsticks, skin removed and trimmed of excess fat	2 kg
3	medium leeks (white and light green parts only), trimmed, washed and thinly sliced	3
1	clove garlic, minced	1
2	large apples, peeled, cored and cut into 1-inch (2.5 cm) pieces	2
½ tsp	salt	2 mL
½ tsp	black pepper	2 mL
½ tsp	dried tarragon	2 mL
1½ cups	apple cider or apple juice	375 mL
1 tbsp	cornstarch	15 mL
1 tbsp	cold water	15 mL
2 tbsp	grainy Dijon mustard	25 mL
	Chopped fresh parsley or tarragon sprigs	

1. Preheat oven to 375°F (190°C). In the casserole, heat oil and butter over medium-high heat. Cook chicken in batches, turning often, for 3 to 5 minutes or until browned on both sides. Transfer chicken to a plate as each batch browns. Add a little more oil or butter to casserole if necessary. Add leeks and garlic; cook, stirring, for 2 to 3 minutes or until leeks are soft but not brown, scraping up any browned bits from bottom of casserole. Stir in apples, salt, pepper and tarragon.

Kitchen Wisdom

To clean leeks, slit them open lengthwise, but do not cut right through. Hold leeks under cold running water, opening them up slightly to wash away grit. Shake leeks to remove excess water.

2. Return chicken to casserole in a single layer; add any juices that have accumulated on the plate. Add apple cider; bring to a boil. Cover and transfer to oven; cook for 30 to 40 minutes or until juices that run out are no longer pink when thickest chicken pieces are pierced with a skewer. Remove chicken to a warm serving platter. With a slotted spoon, arrange leeks and apples around chicken. Keep warm.

3. In a small bowl, combine cornstarch and water; stir until smooth. Add to cooking juices in casserole; bring to a boil over medium-high heat. Boil, whisking constantly, for 1 minute or until sauce is smooth and slightly thickened. Add mustard; whisk well. If desired, season to taste with additional salt and pepper. Spoon sauce over chicken; serve garnished with parsley.

Lemon roast chicken thighs

Serves 6

Sometimes it takes only the simplest of marinades to add flavor to a dish. In this case, the magic comes from lemon, olive oil, balsamic vinegar and garlic.

I prefer to use meaty chicken thighs for this recipe, as they are juicier and less likely to dry out at high temperatures. The appearance of the chicken is better if you leave the skin on — it develops a wondrous crispness — but you can remove it if you prefer. If the chicken thighs are hefty, you may only need 6; otherwise, buy a few more to be sure you have enough.

• Large shallow nonreactive baking dish

¼ cup	fresh lemon juice	50 mL
2 tbsp	olive oil	25 mL
2 tbsp	balsamic vinegar	25 mL
2	cloves garlic, minced	2
2 tsp	grated lemon zest	10 mL
6 to 12	chicken thighs, trimmed of excess fat	6 to 12
½ tsp	salt	2 mL
½ tsp	black pepper	2 mL
	Chopped fresh parsley	

1. In the baking dish, whisk together lemon juice, olive oil, vinegar, garlic and lemon zest. Add chicken thighs; turn to coat well. Refrigerate, covered, for at least 1 hour or up to 24 hours, turning occasionally.

2. When ready to cook, preheat oven to 425°F (220°C). Remove chicken thighs from marinade, shaking off excess. Arrange thighs on oiled rack in a shallow roasting pan (line roasting pan with foil for easy clean up); sprinkle with salt and pepper. Bake for 25 to 35 minutes or until skin is crisp and golden, and juices that run out are no longer pink when thickest thigh is pierced with a skewer. Transfer to a warm platter; serve garnished with parsley.

> **Make Ahead**
> Chicken thighs must be marinated in the refrigerator for at least 1 hour or up to 24 hours.

Garlic-herb chicken with balsamic glaze

Serves 6

This is one of those dishes that is very easy to prepare but somehow has that restaurant-dinner quality that will impress the you-know-what out of your guests. To be really trendy, serve the chicken breasts with one of the less garlicky mashed potato variations on page 121 and a green salad. For best flavor, look for air-chilled chicken breasts.

Kitchen Wisdom

Use a silicon pastry brush when applying the vinegar glaze, then toss it in the dishwasher afterward.

• Heavy baking sheet lined with lightly oiled foil

6	bone-in, skin-on chicken breasts (about 4 lbs/2 kg)	6
1	package (5 oz/150 g) French soft cheese with garlic and herbs (such as Boursin), cut into 6 pieces	1
¼ cup	balsamic vinegar	50 mL
¼ cup	olive oil	50 mL
¾ tsp	salt	4 mL
¾ tsp	black pepper	4 mL
	Fresh herb sprigs (parsley, basil, thyme, oregano and/or tarragon)	

1. Preheat oven to 400°F (200°C). With your fingers, carefully lift skin from each chicken breast to form a pocket between skin and flesh. Place 1 piece of cheese under skin of each chicken breast; massage skin to spread cheese evenly. Place chicken breasts in a single layer on prepared baking sheet.

2. In a small bowl, whisk together balsamic vinegar and oil. Generously brush chicken breasts with half the vinegar mixture; sprinkle with salt and pepper.

3. Bake for 20 minutes. Whisk remaining vinegar mixture; brush generously over chicken breasts. Continue to bake for 20 to 30 minutes or until golden brown and juices that run out are no longer pink when thickest chicken breast is pierced with a skewer. Serve chicken on a bed of fresh herbs on a warm serving platter.

> ### Make Ahead
> Massage cheese into the chicken breasts then refrigerate, covered, for up to 24 hours.

Lindos chicken

The last vacation of my mother's life was to Lindos, on the Greek island of Rhodes, with my sister Lucy and her family. She had an idyllic time — and especially enjoyed shopping for local foods. The area in which they stayed was blessed with a terrific butcher shop, which, although run by the local garbage collector, was nonetheless spotlessly clean.

When not sampling the menus of the local tavernas, Mum and Lucy would cook up a storm in their rented villa. This is my version of one of the dishes they created. My mother would turn in her grave at the addition of olive oil (the one ingredient she loathed above all others), but it does make the dish more authentically Greek. Serve with rice or mashed potatoes and a green salad.

• Large shallow nonreactive dish

Marinade

2	lemons	2
1/2 cup	dry white wine	125 mL
1 tbsp	liquid honey	15 mL
2	cloves garlic, thinly sliced	2
1 tbsp	chopped fresh oregano (or 1 1/2 tsp/7 mL dried)	15 mL

Chicken

8	chicken thighs, skin removed and trimmed of excess fat (about 2 1/2 lbs/1.25 kg)	8
2 tbsp	olive oil	25 mL
1	large onion, coarsely chopped	1
1/4 tsp	salt	1 mL
1/4 tsp	black pepper	1 mL
1	red bell pepper, seeded and cut into strips	1
1 cup	pitted black olives	250 mL
2 tsp	cold water	10 mL
1 tsp	cornstarch	5 mL
	Fresh oregano leaves or parsley sprigs	

1. **Marinade:** With a lemon zester or using the smallest holes on a cheese grater, grate zest from 1 lemon; set aside. With a sharp vegetable peeler or knife, cut four 2-inch (5 cm) strips of zest from other lemon. Cut both lemons in half; squeeze juice into the dish. Whisk in lemon zest strips, white wine, honey, garlic and oregano.

2. **Chicken:** Add chicken thighs, turning to coat well. Refrigerate, covered, for at least 8 hours or up to 24 hours, turning thighs occasionally.

Kitchen Wisdom

Don't use canned olives for this recipe. Look for kalamata or other black olives in the deli section of your supermarket. To remove pits, use an olive or cherry pitter or simply smash each olive with the flat side of a large knife, then carefully peel the flesh from the pit.

The easiest way to remove skin from chicken thighs is to grasp the edge of the skin with a piece of paper towel and peel it off.

3. Remove chicken thighs from marinade, shaking off excess. Reserve marinade. In a large skillet, heat oil over medium-high heat. Cook chicken in batches, turning often, for 3 to 5 minutes or until browned on both sides. (Chicken will not be cooked through.) Transfer chicken to a plate as each batch browns.

4. Drain off all but 1 tbsp (15 mL) fat from skillet. Add onion; cook over medium-high heat, stirring, for 4 to 6 minutes or until golden brown. Return chicken to skillet along with reserved marinade and any juices that have accumulated on the plate; sprinkle with salt and pepper. Bring to a boil over medium-high heat. Reduce heat to medium-low; simmer, covered, for 30 minutes.

5. Scatter red pepper and olives over chicken. Simmer, covered, for 10 minutes or until pepper is tender and juices that run out are no longer pink when thickest thigh is pierced with a skewer. If desired, season to taste with additional salt and pepper. With a slotted spoon, transfer chicken and vegetables to a warm shallow serving dish; keep warm.

6. In a small bowl, whisk together water and cornstarch until smooth; add to sauce in skillet. Bring to a boil over high heat, whisking constantly. Reduce heat to medium-low; simmer, stirring often, for 1 to 2 minutes or until sauce is bubbly and slightly thickened. Pour over chicken and vegetables. Serve garnished with reserved grated lemon zest and oregano.

Make Ahead
Marinate the chicken, refrigerated, for at least 8 hours or up to 24 hours.

Easy roast turkey

Serves 8 to 10

*If you're nervous
about cooking a
turkey for Christmas
or Thanksgiving, try
this foolproof recipe.
Be warned, however;
you may find yourself
hosting the celebrations
every year.*

• Shallow roasting pan with oiled rack

Turkey

1	bunch fresh thyme	1
1	fresh turkey (about 14 lbs/6.5 kg), giblets and neck reserved for stock	1
1	onion, unpeeled, cut into quarters	1
1	apple, unpeeled, cut into quarters	1
1	lemon, cut in half	1
1 tsp	salt	5 mL
1 tsp	black pepper	5 mL
2 tsp	dried thyme	10 mL
6	slices bacon	6

Giblet Stock

3 cups	water	750 mL
	Turkey giblets and neck	
1	small onion, unpeeled and cut into quarters	1
2	sun-dried tomatoes	2
1 tbsp	dried porcini mushrooms	15 mL
1 tsp	whole black peppercorns	5 mL
½ tsp	salt	2 mL
1	bay leaf	1

Gravy

3 tbsp	cornstarch	45 mL
3 tbsp	cold water	45 mL
1 cup	red wine	250 mL

Kitchen Wisdom

Cooking the turkey upside down for the first 2 hours ensures the breast meat stays moist.

Wear clean oven mitts when turning the turkey over halfway through roasting, then be sure to toss them in the laundry immediately afterward to avoid contaminating other utensils with uncooked turkey juices.

1. **Turkey:** Preheat oven to 325°F (160°C). Reserving a few sprigs of thyme for garnish, put half of remaining bunch into turkey's body cavity, along with half onion, apple and lemon. Reserve remaining lemon half. Put remaining thyme, onion and apple in neck cavity. Place turkey breast-side down on rack in roasting pan; sprinkle with $\frac{1}{2}$ tsp (2 mL) each salt and pepper. Roast, uncovered, for 2 hours, basting occasionally with cooking juices.

2. Wearing clean oven mitts, turn turkey breast-side up. Squeeze juice from reserved lemon half over turkey breast; sprinkle with dried thyme and remaining salt and pepper. Lay bacon slices across turkey. Roast, basting occasionally with cooking juices in roasting pan, for $1\frac{1}{2}$ to 2 hours or until a meat thermometer inserted into thickest part of thigh registers 185°F (85°C) and juices that run out of thigh are no longer pink. Remove turkey to a warm serving platter; tent loosely with foil. Let stand in a warm place for 20 minutes before carving. Remove rack from roasting pan. Pour cooking juices from pan into a bowl; place in freezer.

3. **Giblet Stock:** While turkey is roasting, prepare giblet stock as in The Ultimate Roast Chicken (see recipe, page 84).

4. **Gravy:** In a small bowl, combine cornstarch and water; stir until smooth. Pour giblet stock and red wine into roasting pan. Bring to a boil over high heat, stirring to scrape up any browned bits from bottom of pan. Whisk cornstarch mixture into gravy; bring to a boil, whisking constantly. Reduce heat to medium-low; simmer, whisking occasionally, for 3 to 5 minutes or until gravy is thickened and smooth.

5. Remove cooking juices from freezer; carefully skim and discard fat that has risen to top. Add juices to gravy, along with any juices that have accumulated under the turkey. If desired, season to taste with additional salt and pepper. Pour gravy into a pitcher. Remove bacon from turkey; garnish with reserved fresh thyme before carving.

Apple-thyme stuffing

Serves 8

Cooking the stuffing separately makes serving roast turkey a snap — no more fishing around inside the bird to make sure everyone gets a share.

Kitchen Wisdom

When preparing celery, don't remove individual stalks — use the whole bunch, slicing it as you need it, starting from the leafy tops. Keeping the root end intact this way helps the celery stay fresh longer.

Make Ahead
Unbaked stuffing can be refrigerated, covered, for up to 24 hours or frozen for up to 1 month. Thaw in the refrigerator overnight then bake as directed in recipe.

• 8-inch (2 L) square baking dish, lightly greased

6	slices bacon, chopped	6
1	large onion, chopped	1
1 cup	chopped celery	250 mL
2	cloves garlic, minced	2
1 tbsp	fresh lemon juice	15 mL
8	slices day-old white bread, crusts removed and cut into $\frac{1}{2}$-inch (1 cm) cubes	8
1	apple, peeled, cored and chopped	1
$\frac{2}{3}$ cup	chopped fresh parsley	150 mL
1	egg, beaten	1
1 tsp	grated lemon zest	5 mL
1 tsp	dried thyme	5 mL
1 tsp	dried savory	5 mL
$\frac{1}{2}$ tsp	salt	2 mL
$\frac{1}{2}$ tsp	black pepper	2 mL

1. Preheat oven to 425°F (220°C). In a skillet over medium-high heat, cook bacon for 3 to 5 minutes or until crisp. With a slotted spoon, remove bacon to a bowl; reserve fat in skillet.

2. Add onion, celery and garlic to skillet. Reduce heat to medium-low; cook, stirring, for 10 minutes or until onion and celery are soft but not brown. Add contents of skillet to bacon. Add lemon juice to skillet, stirring to scrape up any browned bits from bottom of skillet. Add lemon juice to bacon mixture.

3. Add bread cubes, apple, $\frac{1}{2}$ cup (125 mL) parsley, egg, lemon zest, thyme, savory, salt and pepper to bacon mixture; stir well. Spoon stuffing into baking dish; cover tightly with foil.

4. Bake for 25 minutes or until stuffing is piping hot. Remove foil; cook for 5 minutes or until top is golden brown. Sprinkle with remaining parsley before serving.

Meat

See also...

Caribbean beef stew

Serves 6 to 8

Don't let the rather long list of ingredients put you off making this stew. It's the easiest in the world to prepare — you don't even have to brown the beef first — and chances are you already have most of the seasonings in your cupboard.

Serve with rice or baked potatoes.

This stew isn't fiery-hot, but if you want to give it more kick, put hot pepper sauce on the table so your guests can add it to taste.

Make Ahead
Stew can be cooked, cooled then refrigerated for up to 2 days. Reheat over medium heat, stirring occasionally, until piping hot and bubbly.

- 16-cup (4 L) Dutch oven or flameproof casserole

1 tbsp	canola oil or vegetable oil	15 mL
1	large onion, chopped	1
1	large green bell pepper, seeded and chopped	1
4	cloves garlic, minced	4
3 lbs	stew beef, trimmed and cut into 1-inch (2.5 cm) cubes	1.5 kg
1/4 cup	all-purpose flour	50 mL
1	can (28 oz/796 mL) diced tomatoes	1
1/4 cup	red wine vinegar	50 mL
2 tbsp	paprika	25 mL
1 tsp	dried oregano	5 mL
1 tsp	ground sage	5 mL
1 tsp	ground ginger	5 mL
1/2 tsp	granulated sugar	2 mL
1/2 tsp	salt	2 mL
1/4 tsp	hot pepper flakes	1 mL
1/2 cup	raisins	125 mL
1/2 cup	drained pimento-stuffed green olives	125 mL
	Fresh sage leaves	

1. Preheat oven to 300°F (150°C). In the Dutch oven, heat oil over medium-high heat. Add onion and green pepper; cook, stirring, for 3 to 5 minutes or until onion is soft but not brown. Add garlic and cook, stirring, for 1 minute. Remove from heat. Add beef. Sprinkle beef with flour and stir to coat beef with flour and onion mixture. Add tomatoes, vinegar, paprika, oregano, sage, ginger, sugar, salt and hot pepper flakes; stir until well combined.

2. Transfer to oven; cook, covered, for 2 1/2 hours. Stir in raisins and olives; cook, covered, for 30 minutes or until beef is tender. Serve garnished with sage.

Molasses-Glazed Salmon on Mesclun (page 68)
Overleaf: Caribbean Beef Stew (this page)

Faheem's beef and tomato curry

Serves 4 to 6

My friend Faheem Ahmad is a terrific cook. Dinner invitations to his place are always snapped up in an instant and there are little or no leftovers at the end of the evening. When this beef curry is on the table, it's usually the first thing to disappear. It's spicy without being fiery — a great introduction for anyone unfamiliar with Pakistani or Indian food.

Kitchen Wisdom

Hot banana peppers resemble bell peppers but are longer and slimmer. They're fairly hot without being too fiery.

Make Ahead
This is a perfect make-ahead dish as it tastes even better after 24 hours.

The curry can be cooked, cooled then refrigerated for up to 2 days. Reheat over medium heat, stirring occasionally, until piping hot and bubbly.

- 12-cup (3 L) Dutch oven or flameproof casserole

1	medium onion, coarsely chopped	1
4	cloves garlic, coarsely chopped	4
1	1-inch (2.5 cm) piece ginger root, coarsely chopped	1
¼ cup	canola oil or vegetable oil	50 mL
1 tbsp	hot curry powder	15 mL
1	can (28 oz/796 mL) diced tomatoes	1
2 tsp	granulated sugar	10 mL
½ tsp	salt	2 mL
2 lbs	stew beef, trimmed of excess fat and cut into 1-inch (2.5 cm) cubes	1 kg
1	hot banana pepper, washed	1
¼ tsp	cayenne pepper (or to taste)	1 mL
¼ cup	chopped fresh coriander	50 mL

1. In a food processor or mini chopper, combine onion, garlic and ginger; process until finely ground. In Dutch oven, heat oil over medium-high heat. Add onion mixture; cook, stirring, for 3 to 5 minutes or until just beginning to brown. Add curry powder; cook, stirring, for 1 minute.

2. Stir in tomatoes, sugar and salt. Increase heat to high; bring to a boil, stirring to scrape up any brown bits from bottom of Dutch oven. Add beef and whole banana pepper. Reduce heat to medium-low; simmer, covered, for 1 ½ hours or until beef is tender.

3. If sauce seems a little thin, increase heat to high. Boil, stirring occasionally, for 8 to 10 minutes or until sauce is reduced and slightly thickened. Discard banana pepper; stir in cayenne pepper. Spoon curry into a warm shallow serving dish. Sprinkle with coriander; serve at once.

Pot roast of beef with wild mushrooms

Serves 6

I much prefer cheaper cuts of beef, such as cross rib, blade or short-rib roasts, because I think they have so much more flavor than more expensive choices. A pot roast like this one needs very little in the way of preparation, after which it happily looks after itself for 2 or 3 hours in the oven. The result is moist and tender meat in an intensely flavored gravy. Serve this with mashed potatoes (any one of the variations on page 121) or with Arpi's Splendid Polenta (see recipe, page 123).

• 12-cup (3 L) Dutch oven or flameproof casserole

1 cup	boiling water	250 mL
1/2 oz	dried porcini mushrooms	15 g
1 tbsp	olive oil	15 mL
1	cross-rib, blade or short-rib beef roast (about 3 lbs/1.5 kg)	1
1/2 tsp	salt	2 mL
1/2 tsp	black pepper	2 mL
8 oz	shallots, peeled but left whole	250 g
1 cup	red wine	250 mL
1 tsp	dried thyme	5 mL
1	bay leaf	1
3 cups	sliced mixed mushrooms (button, shiitake, portobello; about 8 oz/250 g)	750 mL
1 tbsp	cornstarch	15 mL
1 tbsp	cold water	15 mL
	Fresh thyme or parsley sprigs	

1. Preheat oven to 325°F (160°C). In a small heatproof bowl, combine boiling water and porcini mushrooms; let stand for 20 minutes. Line a sieve with paper towels; drain porcini mushrooms through sieve, reserving soaking liquid. Rinse porcini mushrooms under running water; pat dry on paper towels. Set aside.

2. In the Dutch oven, heat oil over medium-high heat. Sprinkle roast with salt and pepper; place in Dutch oven. Cook, turning often, for 3 to 5 minutes or until browned on all sides. Remove roast to a plate.

3. Add shallots to the fat remaining in Dutch oven; cook, stirring, for 3 to 5 minutes or until golden brown. Add porcini mushrooms, reserved soaking liquid, red wine, thyme and bay leaf. Bring to a boil, stirring to scrape up any browned bits from bottom of Dutch oven. Return beef to Dutch oven; cover with lid. Transfer to oven; cook for $2\frac{1}{2}$ hours. Remove from oven; add sliced mushrooms, stirring to combine with cooking juices. Return to oven; cook, covered, for 30 minutes or until beef is very tender and mushrooms are cooked. Remove beef to a large plate. Cover loosely with foil; keep warm.

4. In a small bowl, whisk together cornstarch and cold water until smooth; add to cooking juices in Dutch oven. Bring to a boil over medium-high heat, stirring constantly. Reduce heat to medium-low; simmer, stirring often, for 2 to 3 minutes or until mushroom gravy has thickened and is smooth. If desired, season to taste with additional salt and pepper; discard bay leaf.

5. Cut beef into thick slices; arrange on a warm serving platter. Drizzle some mushroom gravy evenly over beef; pour remaining gravy into a warm serving bowl. Garnish beef with thyme. Serve at once.

Flank steak times three

Serves 6

Flank steak is one of my favorite cuts of beef. It's reasonably priced and needs little preparation apart from being anointed with a good marinade. Here I've included recipes for three delicious marinades — take your pick.

Flank steak should be marinated for at least 8 or up to 24 hours. Serve it thinly sliced across the grain with a potato dish, such as Potato-Tomato Temptation (see recipe, page 122), and a green salad, such as Escarole Salad with Olives (see recipe, page 146).

It's worth investing in a bottle of dry sherry for the Asian marinade. Even if it's not your favorite tipple, you can refrigerate what's left in the bottle and use it for dishes such as Chinese Braised Pork (see recipe, page 106) or Roasted Red Pepper and Garlic Soup (see recipe, page 38).

• Large nonreactive baking dish

1	flank steak (1½ to 2 lbs/750 g to 1 kg), trimmed of excess fat	1

Asian Marinade

¼ cup	dry sherry	50 mL
¼ cup	soya sauce	50 mL
1 tbsp	oyster sauce	15 mL
1 tbsp	sesame oil	15 mL
2	cloves garlic, minced	2
1 tsp	minced ginger root	5 mL
1 tsp	Asian chili sauce	5 mL

Indian Marinade

1 cup	plain yogurt	250 mL
1	small onion, quartered	1
2	cloves garlic, sliced	2
1	1-inch (2.5 cm) piece ginger root, coarsely chopped	1
1	small hot pepper, seeded and coarsely chopped	1
1 tsp	allspice	5 mL
1 tsp	ground cumin	5 mL
1 tsp	ground coriander	5 mL

Tex-Mex Marinade

1 cup	salsa (mild, medium or hot)	250 mL
¼ cup	chopped fresh coriander	50 mL
1 tbsp	drained, minced pickled jalapeño peppers	15 mL
1 tsp	ground cumin	5 mL
1 tsp	dried oregano	5 mL
	Watercress	

Kitchen Wisdom

Flank steak is best served rare or medium-rare, so try not to overcook it. The cooking times in this recipe will vary depending on whether you cook the steak indoors or out and, if you're cooking on an outside barbecue, what the weather is like the day you grill (a breezy day may lengthen the cooking time a little.)

When handling hot peppers, always wear rubber or plastic gloves and avoid touching your face. Wash your knife and cutting board in hot soapy water immediately afterward.

Sesame oil is a vibrantly flavored oil that frequently appears in Asian recipes. It has a strong flavor so use sparingly. Look for sesame oil in the Asian section of your supermarket. It will be labeled as pure sesame oil or as a blend of sesame and soybean oils; either type is fine for this recipe. For a quick vegetable dish to accompany meat, fish or poultry, try tossing cooked broccoli or green beans in a little sesame oil then sprinkling them with toasted sesame seeds.

1. With a sharp knife, score steak on both sides at 2-inch (5 cm) intervals, taking care not to cut right through meat. Set aside.

2. **Asian Marinade:** In the baking dish, whisk together sherry, soya sauce, oyster sauce, sesame oil, garlic, ginger and chili sauce. Add steak, turning to coat both sides with marinade.

   Indian Marinade: In a food processor or blender, combine yogurt, onion, garlic, ginger, hot pepper, allspice, cumin and coriander; process until fairly smooth. Pour mixture into baking dish. Add steak, turning to coat both sides with marinade.

   Tex-Mex Marinade: In the baking dish, stir together salsa, coriander, jalapeño peppers, cumin and oregano. Add steak, turning to coat both sides with marinade.

3. Refrigerate flank steak, covered, for at least 8 hours or up to 24 hours, turning occasionally. Let stand at room temperature for 30 minutes before cooking.

4. Preheat barbecue to medium-high or heat a heavy ridged grill pan on stovetop over medium-high heat. Remove steak from marinade; pat dry with paper towels. Grill for 3 to 6 minutes per side for medium-rare.

5. Transfer steak to a cutting board; cover loosely with foil and let stand in a warm place for 10 minutes. Using a sharp knife, cut steak crosswise (across the grain) into thin slices. Arrange on a warm serving platter; garnish with watercress. Serve at once.

Make Ahead
Flank steak can be marinated in the refrigerator for up to 24 hours.

Foolproof roast beef

Serves 8

It's hard to beat a really good roast beef — and even harder to screw it up when you use this wonderfully simple recipe.

When ordering the prime-rib roast, ask your butcher to separate the meat from the ribs then tie them back together. The bones will add flavor to the meat as it cooks then, once the roast is ready, just snip the strings, discard the ribs and you have a boneless roast that's easy to carve.

• Shallow roasting pan

Rub

1	prime-rib roast, about 6 lbs (3 kg)	1
1	clove garlic, crushed with the flat blade of a large knife	1
1	onion, thickly sliced	1
½ tsp	black pepper	2 mL
¼ cup	grainy Dijon mustard	50 mL
2 tsp	fresh thyme leaves (or 1 tsp/5 mL dried)	10 mL

Gravy

2 tbsp	all-purpose flour	25 mL
2 cups	beef stock	500 mL
¼ tsp	salt	1 mL
	Fresh thyme sprigs	

1. **Rub:** Preheat oven to 475°F (250°C). Rub roast all over with garlic; place garlic in roasting pan, along with onion. Sprinkle roast with black pepper. In a small bowl, stir together mustard and thyme leaves; spread over roast. Place roast bone-side down on top of onion and garlic. Roast, uncovered, for 20 minutes. Reduce oven temperature to 325°F (160°C); cook for 2½ to 3 hours or until a meat thermometer inserted in roast (but not the touching the bones) registers 120°F (48°C) for rare or 140°F (60°C) for medium. Remove roast to a cutting board; tent loosely with foil and let stand in a warm place for 20 minutes before carving.

Using a meat thermometer is the most accurate way of establishing whether a roast is done to your taste. For an accurate reading with a bone-in roast, be sure the shaft of the thermometer does not touch any bones.

2. **Gravy:** Drain off all but 2 tbsp (25 mL) fat from roasting pan; reserve onion and garlic in pan. Sprinkle flour evenly over fat remaining in pan; stir until no lumps of flour remain. Place roasting pan on stovetop; cook over medium-high heat for 1 minute, stirring constantly. Gradually whisk in stock; bring to a boil, stirring constantly. Reduce heat to low; simmer for 5 minutes or until gravy has thickened and is smooth. If desired, season to taste with salt and additional pepper. Strain gravy through a sieve into a pitcher.

3. If your butcher has separated the meat from the bones (see note, at left on facing page) snip strings on roast, remove bones and slice meat thinly. Arrange meat on a warm serving platter; garnish with thyme. Serve with gravy.

Make Ahead
The roast can be rubbed with garlic and pepper, covered with the mustard mixture then refrigerated, covered, for up to 24 hours. Let the beef stand at room temperature for 30 minutes before roasting.

Roast pork loin with spiced pear stuffing

Serves 6 to 8

Pork and applesauce has long been a happy marriage of flavors, but pork goes just as well with other fall fruit, such as pears. To ensure pork is moist and juicy, roast the loin only until it registers 160°F (70°C) on a meat thermometer.

• Shallow roasting pan

2	cloves garlic, minced	2
2 tsp	minced ginger root	10 mL
¾ tsp	salt	4 mL
¾ tsp	black pepper	4 mL
¾ tsp	ground cinnamon	4 mL
1	boneless center-cut pork loin roast, about 3 lbs (1.5 kg)	1
3	ripe pears, peeled, cored and thinly sliced	3
1 cup	dry white wine	250 mL
1 cup	chicken stock	250 mL
½ cup	whipping (35%) cream	125 mL
	Slices of unpeeled pear, brushed with lemon juice	

1. Preheat oven to 325°F (160°C). In a small bowl, stir together garlic, ginger and ½ tsp (2 mL) each salt, pepper and cinnamon. Remove strings from pork; open up roast like a book. Spread garlic mixture over the inside of one half of roast. Arrange one-third of pear slices evenly over garlic mixture. Close pork; re-tie at intervals along its length.

2. In a small bowl, stir together remaining salt, pepper and cinnamon; rub over outside of pork. Spread remaining pear slices over base of roasting pan. Place pork on top of pears; pour wine and ½ cup (125 mL) stock into pan. Roast, uncovered, for 2 hours or until a meat thermometer inserted into pork registers 160°F (70°C).

3. Remove pork to a cutting board; tent loosely with foil and let stand in a warm place for 10 minutes. Add cream and remaining stock to pear mixture in roasting pan. Place on stovetop; bring to a boil over high heat, stirring to scrape up any browned bits from bottom of pan. Boil, stirring occasionally, for 2 to 3 minutes or until gravy thickens slightly. Whisk in any juices that have accumulated under pork. If desired, season to taste with additional salt and pepper. Pour gravy into a warm pitcher.

4. Cut pork into slices; arrange on a warm platter. Garnish with unpeeled pear slices. Serve with gravy.

Chinese braised pork

Serves 4 to 6

Here's a recipe shared by Rose Murray — a very good friend (and favorite traveling companion) of mine.

Country-style pork ribs (also called pork loin ribs or Texas ribs) lend themselves well to Asian flavors. Serve this easy braise with rice and a colorful stir-fry of whatever vegetables you happen to have in your refrigerator. Don't be alarmed by the amount of garlic in this recipe; long, slow cooking renders it quite mild.

- Shallow nonreactive baking dish
- Large deep skillet

⅓ cup	low-sodium soya sauce	75 mL
3 tbsp	rice wine or dry sherry	45 mL
3 tbsp	hoisin sauce	45 mL
5	cloves garlic, minced	5
2 tbsp	minced ginger root	25 mL
1½ tsp	sesame oil	7 mL
2 lbs	country-style pork ribs, in one piece	1 kg
1 tbsp	canola oil or vegetable oil	15 mL
1½ cups	chicken stock	375 mL
1 tbsp	granulated sugar	15 mL
¼ tsp	hot pepper flakes	1 mL
2 tbsp	cold water	25 mL
1 tbsp	cornstarch	15 mL
	Chopped green onions	

1. In the baking dish, whisk together soya sauce, rice wine, hoisin sauce, garlic, ginger and sesame oil. Add pork, turning to coat well. Let stand, covered, at room temperature for 30 minutes, turning pork occasionally.

2. Remove pork from dish, reserving marinade and scraping garlic and ginger off pork back into marinade; pat dry with paper towels. In a skillet, heat oil over medium-high heat. Add pork and cook, turning once, for 3 to 5 minutes or until browned on both sides. Remove pork to a plate.

3. Add reserved marinade to skillet, along with chicken stock, sugar and hot pepper flakes. Bring to a boil over high heat, stirring to scrape up any browned bits from bottom of skillet.

4. Return pork to skillet, basting to coat with sauce. Reduce heat to medium-low; simmer, covered, for $1\frac{1}{2}$ to 2 hours or until pork is tender, turning pork occasionally and basting with sauce. Remove pork to a cutting board; tent loosely with foil and let stand in a warm place for 10 minutes.

5. In a small bowl, whisk together water and cornstarch until smooth; add to sauce in skillet. Increase heat to medium-high; simmer, whisking constantly, for 1 to 2 minutes or until sauce has thickened and is smooth. Cut pork into serving-size portions. Whisk any juices that have accumulated under pork into sauce in skillet. Arrange pork on a warm platter; pour sauce over pork. Serve garnished with green onions.

Maple-mustard glazed pork tenderloins

Serves 4 to 6

Pork tenderloin is a great choice for entertaining — there's no waste and the lean meat takes very little time to cook. For best results, use a good-quality Worcestershire sauce, such as Lea & Perrins. Be sure not to overcook the pork or it will be tough; at 150°F (65°C) it should still be very slightly pink inside.

Kitchen Wisdom

If your skillet doesn't have an ovenproof handle, wrap the handle in a double layer of foil before putting it in the oven.

Try using grainy Dijon mustard — it makes the sauce look even more attractive.

- Large shallow nonreactive baking dish
- Large heavy ovenproof skillet or shallow flameproof casserole, lightly oiled

Marinade

½ cup	Worcestershire sauce	125 mL
1 tsp	hot pepper sauce	5 mL
1	clove garlic, minced	1
2	large pork tenderloins (each about 1 lb/500 g), trimmed of excess fat	2

Maple-Mustard Glaze

1 cup	chicken stock	250 mL
2 tbsp	maple syrup	25 mL
2 tbsp	Dijon mustard	25 mL
Pinch	salt	Pinch
Pinch	black pepper	Pinch
	Watercress or fresh sage sprigs	

1. **Marinade:** In the baking dish, whisk together Worcestershire sauce, hot pepper sauce and garlic. Add tenderloins, turning to coat well. Marinate for 1 hour at room temperature, turning tenderloins once, or refrigerate, covered, for up to 24 hours, turning tenderloins occasionally.

2. Preheat oven to 475°F (250°C). Heat skillet over medium-high heat. Remove tenderloins from marinade, shaking off excess; reserve marinade. Put tenderloins in skillet and cook over medium-high heat, turning often, for 2 to 3 minutes or until browned on all sides. Transfer skillet to oven; cook for 18 to 20 minutes or until a meat thermometer inserted into thickest part of tenderloins registers 155°F (68°C). Wearing oven mitts, remove skillet from oven. Remove tenderloins to a cutting board; tent loosely with foil and let stand in a warm place for 5 minutes.

3. Maple-Mustard Glaze: Meanwhile, in a 2-cup (500 mL) liquid measure, whisk together stock, maple syrup, mustard, salt, pepper and 2 tbsp (25 mL) reserved marinade; add to skillet. Bring to a boil over high heat, stirring to scrape up any brown bits from bottom of skillet. Boil for 5 to 7 minutes or until stock mixture is reduced to about $\frac{3}{4}$ cup (175 mL) and has thickened slightly. Add any juices that have accumulated under pork on cutting board. If desired, season to taste with additional salt and pepper.

4. Cut each tenderloin diagonally into $\frac{1}{2}$-inch (1 cm) slices. Arrange on a warm platter; drizzle with glaze. Serve garnished with watercress.

Make Ahead
Pork tenderloins should be marinated in the refrigerator for at least 1 hour or up to 24 hours.

Pork braised with fennel and orange

Serves 4 to 6

The flavors of fennel and orange add Mediterranean flair to this easy braise.

Using boneless pork steaks cuts the cooking time to well under 1 hour.

Serve in wide bowls with rice, mashed potatoes or crusty bread.

• 12-cup (3 L) Dutch oven or flameproof casserole

¼ cup	olive oil	50 mL
2 lbs	boneless pork steaks, trimmed of excess fat and cut into 1-inch (2.5 cm) cubes	1 kg
1	large onion, thinly sliced	1
1	head fennel (about 1 lb/500 g), trimmed and thinly sliced crosswise	1
2	cloves garlic, minced	2
1	large orange	1
1 cup	chicken stock	250 mL
2 tbsp	tomato paste	25 mL
½ cup	chopped sun-dried tomatoes	125 mL
1 tbsp	minced fresh rosemary leaves (or 1 tsp/5 mL crumbled dried)	15 mL
¼ tsp	salt	1 mL
¼ tsp	black pepper	1 mL
	Fresh rosemary sprigs or chopped fresh parsley	

1. In the Dutch oven, heat 1 tbsp (15 mL) oil over medium-high heat. Cook pork in batches, turning often, for 3 to 5 minutes or until pork is browned but not cooked through. Remove pork to a plate as each batch browns, adding more oil to Dutch oven if necessary.

2. In the Dutch oven, heat 1 tbsp (15 mL) oil over medium-high heat. Add onion, fennel and garlic; cook, stirring, for 3 to 5 minutes or until onion is soft but not browned.

Kitchen Wisdom

Fennel, sometimes called anise, resembles thick, bulbous celery and has a sweetish, aniseed flavor. It can be eaten raw or cooked, and is a great addition to coleslaw or other vegetable salads.

3. Grate zest and squeeze juice from orange. In a 2-cup (500 mL) liquid measure, whisk together stock, orange juice and tomato paste; add to Dutch oven, along with orange zest, sun-dried tomatoes, rosemary, salt and pepper. Bring to a boil over high heat, stirring to scrape up any brown bits from bottom of Dutch oven.

4. Return pork to Dutch oven, along with juices that have accumulated on the plate. Reduce heat to low; simmer, covered, for 20 minutes or until pork and vegetables are tender. If desired, season to taste with additional salt and pepper. Serve garnished with fresh rosemary.

> ### Make Ahead
> The braise can be cooked, cooled then refrigerated for up to 2 days. Reheat over medium heat, stirring occasionally, until piping hot and bubbly.

Easy skillet lamb shanks

Serves 6

Here's the ultimate in comfort food: meaty, succulent lamb shanks in a flavorful sauce that need little accompaniment apart from creamy mashed potatoes or crusty bread, and a green salad.

Lamb shanks from New Zealand are available in most large supermarkets; look for them in the frozen meat department. If your supermarket doesn't have them, they should — so kick up a fuss!

• Deep skillet with lid *or* Dutch oven
• large enough to hold lamb shanks in one layer

1 tbsp	canola oil or vegetable oil	15 mL
6	lamb shanks (about 3½ lbs/ 1.75 kg in total), thawed if frozen, patted dry	6
2	large onions, sliced	2
1½ cups	beef stock	375 mL
2 tbsp	tomato paste	25 mL
2 tbsp	mint jelly	25 mL
1 tbsp	Worcestershire sauce	15 mL
1 tbsp	balsamic vinegar	15 mL
1 tsp	dried rosemary	5 mL
¼ tsp	salt	1 mL
¼ tsp	black pepper	1 mL
	Chopped fresh parsley	

1. In the skillet, heat oil over medium-high heat. Cook lamb shanks in batches, turning often, for 3 to 5 minutes or until browned on all sides. Remove shanks to a plate as each batch browns.

2. Add onions to oil remaining in skillet; cook over medium heat, stirring, for 4 to 6 minutes or until onions are golden brown. Stir in stock, tomato paste, mint jelly, Worcestershire sauce, vinegar, rosemary, salt and pepper. Increase heat to high; bring to a boil, scraping up any brown bits from bottom of skillet.

3. Return lamb shanks to skillet, along with any juices that have accumulated on plate, arranging shanks in a single layer and spooning some of the sauce over each. Reduce heat to low; simmer, tightly covered, basting and turning lamb shanks occasionally, for 1½ hours or until lamb shanks are very tender.

4. With a slotted spoon, remove lamb shanks to a warm serving dish; keep warm. Bring contents of skillet to a boil over high heat; boil, stirring occasionally, for 5 minutes or until sauce is reduced in volume and slightly thickened. Spoon over lamb shanks; serve sprinkled with parsley.

Variation

Replace the mint jelly with red currant jelly and add 1 tsp (5 mL) dried thyme along with the rosemary. If you prefer, substitute 3 lbs (1.5 kg) boneless lamb shoulder, cut into 1-inch (2.5 cm) cubes, for the lamb shanks, and cook for just 1 hour.

Make Ahead

Lamb shanks can be cooked, cooled then refrigerated for up to 2 days. Reheat, covered, in a 350°F (180°C) oven for 45 to 60 minutes or until piping hot and bubbly.

Apricot-stuffed leg of lamb

Serves 6

If you can, buy a "tunnel-boned" leg of lamb (it will be marked as such on the label). This is a tidy roast, from which the bone at the center of the leg has been removed, leaving an empty tube that's ideal for stuffing. A regular boned leg of lamb will taste as good; it's just messier to stuff.

• Shallow roasting pan with oiled rack

Stuffing

1 tbsp	butter	15 mL
1/2 cup	finely chopped shallots	125 mL
1/2 tsp	dried thyme	2 mL
3	slices day-old bread, crusts removed and cut into 1/2-inch (1 cm) cubes	3
1/2 cup	chopped dried apricots	125 mL
1 tbsp	maple syrup	15 mL
1/2 tsp	salt	2 mL
1/2 tsp	black pepper	2 mL
1	egg, beaten	1
1	boneless lamb leg roast, about 3 lbs (1.5 kg)	1

Gravy

1 cup	dry white wine	250 mL
1 tbsp	cornstarch	15 mL
1 cup	chicken stock	250 mL
1 to 2 tbsp	apricot jam	15 to 25 mL
1/4 tsp	salt	1 mL
1/4 tsp	black pepper	1 mL
	Fresh thyme sprigs	
	Fresh apricots (optional)	

1. **Stuffing:** Preheat oven to 450°F (230°C). In a skillet, heat butter over medium heat. Add shallots and thyme; cook, stirring, for 2 to 3 minutes or until soft but not brown. Remove from heat; transfer mixture to a bowl. Add bread cubes to bowl; stir to coat well. Add apricots, maple syrup and 1/4 tsp (1 mL) each salt and pepper; stir well. Set aside to cool to room temperature. Stir in egg.

2. If using a "tunnel-boned" leg of lamb (see note, at left on facing page), pack stuffing into tunnel. Tie with kitchen string in a criss-cross fashion as you would a parcel. If using regular boned leg of lamb, open lamb like a book. Spread stuffing over one half of lamb; replace other half of lamb over stuffing. Tie with kitchen string as above.

3. Place lamb on rack in roasting pan; sprinkle with remaining salt and pepper. Roast, uncovered, for 15 minutes. Reduce oven temperature to 350°F (180°C). Roast for 1 hour and 15 minutes or until a meat thermometer inserted in lamb registers 130°F (55°C) for medium-rare, or until done to taste. Remove lamb to a cutting board; tent loosely with foil and let stand in a warm place.

4. **Gravy:** Remove rack from roasting pan; pour off any excess fat. Pour wine into pan; bring to a boil on stovetop over high heat, stirring to scrape up any browned bits from bottom of pan. Boil until wine is reduced to about $1/2$ cup (125 mL). Strain through a sieve into a small bowl; return liquid to roasting pan, discarding any solids.

5. In the same small bowl, whisk together cornstarch and $1/4$ cup (50 mL) chicken stock; add to liquid in pan, along with remaining chicken stock. Bring to a boil, whisking constantly. Reduce heat to medium-low; whisk in 1 tbsp (15 mL) apricot jam, salt and pepper. Simmer, whisking constantly, until gravy is smooth and slightly thickened. Taste and add more jam if necessary. If desired, season to taste with additional salt and pepper. Pour gravy into a pitcher.

6. Cut lamb into slices. Arrange on a warm serving platter; garnish with thyme sprigs and fresh apricots. Serve with gravy.

> **Make Ahead**
> The stuffing can be refrigerated, covered, for up to 24 hours. Do not stuff the lamb until just before cooking.

Tapenade-crusted lamb racks

Serves 4

Roast lamb in less than 30 minutes? It's possible if you serve lamb racks, those neat strips of chops that are available in the frozen meat section of your supermarket. They're perfect for entertaining — easily prepared and quick to cook. For a larger crowd, simply double the recipe.

In this recipe, lamb racks are treated to a coating of tapenade, a traditional French olive paste that's usually served atop slices of toasted baguette.

For best results, cook lamb so that it's still pink in the middle. If possible, buy frozen lamb racks that have been "frenched," or had the bones cleaned of excess fat.

Kitchen Wisdom

Don't use canned olives for this recipe; the flavor won't be nearly as good. Look for kalamata or other black olives in the deli section of your supermarket. To remove pits, use an olive or cherry pitter or simply smash each olive with the flat side of a large knife, then carefully peel the flesh from the pit.

• Rimmed baking sheet or shallow roasting pan

1	lemon	1
½ cup	pitted black olives	125 mL
2 tbsp	drained capers	25 mL
1 tbsp	olive oil	15 mL
1	clove garlic, sliced	1
1 tsp	fresh thyme leaves (or ½ tsp/2 mL dried)	5 mL
2	frenched lamb racks, about 1 lb 6 oz (620 g) in total	2
	Fresh thyme sprigs	

1. Preheat oven to 450°F (230°C). Cut 4 thin slices from lemon; set aside. Squeeze 2 tsp (10 mL) juice from rest of lemon. In a mini chopper, food processor or blender, combine lemon juice, olives, capers, olive oil, garlic and thyme; process until finely minced and well combined.

2. Place lamb racks, meaty-side up, on baking sheet; spread olive mixture over top of each lamb rack. Roast, uncovered, for 20 minutes (rare), 25 minutes (medium-rare), or until a meat thermometer inserted into meaty part of lamb (not touching any bones) registers 120°F or 130°F (48°C or 55°C).

3. Remove lamb from oven; transfer to a warm serving platter. Let stand, loosely covered with foil, for 10 minutes. To serve, slice lamb between bones into individual chops. Serve garnished with reserved lemon slices and fresh thyme.

> **Make Ahead**
> Tapenade can be refrigerated, covered, for up to 2 days.

Side dishes

Not-just-mashed potatoes

Serves 6

Mashed potatoes have come of age and you'll find ambrosial mixtures like this one in all the best restaurants.

Kitchen Wisdom

Celery root, also known as celeriac, is a round, knobby vegetable with a distinct celery-like flavor. Don't prepare it too far in advance of cooking or it will turn brown.

Never use a food processor or blender to make mashed potatoes; you'll end up with something resembling wallpaper paste. Use either an electric mixer, taking care not to overmix, or mash them the old-fashioned way with a potato masher.

About 4 medium potatoes weigh 1½ lbs (750 g).

1½ lbs	potatoes, peeled and cut into 2-inch (5 cm) chunks	750 g
1	celery root (about 1 lb/500 g), peeled and cut into 1-inch (2.5 cm) chunks	1
4	cloves garlic, peeled but left whole	4
¼ tsp	salt	1 mL
½ cup	whipping (35%) cream	125 mL
2 tbsp	butter	25 mL
¼ tsp	black pepper	1 mL
¼ cup	chopped fresh parsley	50 mL

1. In a large saucepan over high heat, combine potatoes, celery root, garlic and just enough cold water to cover vegetables. Add salt; bring to a boil. Reduce heat to medium-low; cook, covered, for 20 to 25 minutes or until vegetables are very tender. Drain well; return vegetables to saucepan. Place over low heat to dry out vegetables slightly, shaking saucepan occasionally to prevent them from sticking. Remove from heat and set aside.

2. Meanwhile, in a large microwaveable bowl, combine cream and butter. Microwave on High for 1 to 2 minutes or until cream is hot and butter has melted. (Alternatively, heat butter and cream in a saucepan over medium heat; pour into a large bowl.) Add celery root and potatoes; mash roughly with a fork.

3. With an electric mixer, beat vegetables and cream mixture until smooth and creamy. (Don't overbeat or vegetables will become gluey.) Add pepper. If desired, season to taste with additional salt and pepper. Stir in parsley. Spoon into a warm serving dish; serve at once.

> **Make Ahead**
> Mashed potatoes can be refrigerated, covered, for up to 3 days. Reheat, covered, in the microwave on High for 6 to 8 minutes, or in a 350°F (180°C) oven for 30 minutes until piping hot.

Indian-style sautéed potatoes

Serves 6

These aromatic potatoes aren't spicy-hot but the combination of Indian flavors gives them an exotic appeal that will make any dinner extra-special.

Kitchen Wisdom

Cardamom is a wonderfully aromatic spice used extensively in Indian cooking. Its mild flavor goes well with both savory and sweet dishes. Try a little added to the filling of your favorite apple pie, in a rice pudding or with any savory rice dish.

About 6 medium potatoes weigh 2 lbs (1 kg).

.

• Large nonstick skillet

¼ cup	canola oil or vegetable oil	50 mL
1 tsp	turmeric	5 mL
1 tsp	ground cumin	5 mL
1 tsp	ground cardamom	5 mL
½ tsp	salt	2 mL
Pinch	cayenne pepper	Pinch
2 lbs	potatoes, scrubbed and cut into ½-inch (1 cm) pieces	1 kg
1	clove garlic, minced	1
1 tsp	minced ginger root	5 mL
¼ cup	chopped fresh coriander	50 mL

1. In the skillet, heat oil, turmeric, cumin, cardamom, salt and cayenne over medium-high heat. Add potatoes; stir to coat well. Cook, stirring occasionally, for 35 to 40 minutes or until potatoes are golden brown and tender.

2. Add garlic and ginger; cook, stirring, for 3 to 5 minutes or until fragrant. (Don't allow garlic to brown or it will taste bitter.) Spoon potatoes into a warm serving dish; sprinkle with coriander. Serve at once.

> **Make Ahead**
> Potatoes can be scrubbed, cut into pieces then refrigerated in a bowl with enough cold water to cover them, for up to 8 hours

Much more mash

Serves 6

For all those potato purists who find my Not-Just-Mashed Potatoes (page 118) a little avant-garde, here's the real McCoy, along with some tempting variations that are well worth trying.

Kitchen Wisdom

About 8 medium potatoes weigh 2½ lbs (1.25 kg).

2½ lbs	baking potatoes, such as Yukon Gold, peeled and cut into 2-inch (5 cm) chunks	1.25 kg
¼ tsp	salt	1 mL
½ cup	milk	125 mL
2 tbsp	butter or olive oil	25 mL
¼ tsp	black pepper	1 mL
	Chopped fresh parsley	

1. In a large saucepan over high heat, combine potatoes and just enough cold water to cover them. Add salt; bring to a boil. Reduce heat to medium-low; cook, covered, for 20 to 25 minutes or until potatoes are very tender. Drain well; return potatoes to saucepan. Place over low heat to dry out potatoes slightly, shaking saucepan occasionally to prevent them from sticking.

2. Meanwhile, in a small microwaveable bowl, heat milk and butter or oil in microwave on High for 1 to 2 minutes or until steaming. (Alternatively, heat milk and butter or oil in a saucepan over medium-high heat until steaming.) Add milk mixture to potatoes; mash roughly with a fork. With an electric mixer, beat potatoes until smooth and creamy. (Don't overbeat or potatoes will become gluey.) Add pepper. If desired, season to taste with additional salt and pepper. Spoon into a warm serving dish. Sprinkle with parsley; serve at once.

> **Make Ahead**
> Mashed potatoes can be refrigerated, covered, for up to 3 days. Reheat, covered, in the microwave on High for 6 to 8 minutes, or in a 350°F (180°C) oven for 30 minutes until piping hot.

Variations

Pesto Potatoes
Omit butter or oil; add $\frac{1}{4}$ cup (50 mL) each pesto and freshly grated Parmesan cheese before beating.

Mustard Mash
Use butter instead of oil; add $\frac{1}{4}$ cup (50 mL) grainy Dijon mustard before beating.

Lemony Mash
Use oil instead of butter; add $\frac{1}{4}$ cup (50 mL) chopped fresh parsley and 1 tbsp (15 mL) finely grated lemon zest before beating.

Cheese and Onion Mash
Use butter instead of oil; add 1 cup (250 mL) shredded Cheddar or Swiss cheese and $\frac{1}{4}$ cup (50 mL) finely chopped green onions before beating.

Posh French Mash
This is called *aligot* in France and is positively *délicieux*. Add 2 peeled cloves of garlic to potatoes before boiling. Drain well, retaining garlic with potatoes. Mash as above, using butter instead of oil and adding 1 cup (250 mL) shredded Gruyère cheese before beating.

Caesar Potatoes
Omit butter or oil; add $\frac{1}{2}$ cup (125 mL) thick Caesar dressing and $\frac{1}{4}$ cup (50 mL) freshly grated Parmesan cheese before beating.

Potato-tomato temptation

Serves 6

This recipe is based on a traditional Scandinavian accompaniment called Jansson's Temptation, which combines potatoes and anchovies. My version of this easy side dish has more of a Mediterranean flavor, with sun-dried tomatoes and basil standing in for the anchovies. Serve with a lighter main course, such as The Ultimate Roast Chicken (see recipe, page 84).

• 8-inch (2 L) square baking dish, buttered

½ cup	chopped sun-dried tomatoes	125 mL
	Boiling water	
2 lbs	potatoes, peeled and cut into ¼-inch (5 mm) slices	1 kg
1 tsp	dried basil	5 mL
½ tsp	salt	2 mL
½ tsp	black pepper	2 mL
1	onion, thinly sliced	1
1	clove garlic, minced	1
½ cup	whipping (35%) cream	125 mL
½ cup	milk	125 mL
1 tbsp	butter, cut into pieces	15 mL
2 tbsp	chopped fresh parsley	25 mL

1. Preheat oven to 375°F (190°C). In a small heatproof bowl, combine sun-dried tomatoes with enough boiling water to cover them; set aside for 20 minutes. Drain well; set aside.

2. Arrange half the potatoes in baking dish. Sprinkle with ½ tsp (2 mL) basil and ¼ tsp (1 mL) each salt and pepper. Top with half the onion and garlic, and all sun-dried tomatoes. Add remaining onions and garlic; sprinkle with remaining basil, salt and pepper. Arrange remaining potatoes on top. Pour cream and milk into dish; scatter butter pieces on top.

3. Bake, covered, for 30 minutes. Uncover; bake for 30 to 40 minutes or until potatoes are tender and top is browned. Sprinkle with parsley; serve at once.

> **Make Ahead**
> Sun-dried tomatoes can be soaked, drained then refrigerated, covered, for up to 24 hours.

Arpi's splendid polenta

Serves 6

From my good friend, Toronto chef Arpi Magyar, comes this heavenly side dish. Rich and creamy, the polenta makes a good substitute for mashed potatoes, or you can treat it as pasta and top it with a hearty tomato or bolognese sauce. I especially like it alongside Pot Roast of Beef with Wild Mushrooms (see recipe, page 98).

Look for cornmeal next to the rice and other grains in your supermarket, or with the breakfast cereals.

Kitchen Wisdom

For a hearty vegetarian main course, serve the polenta topped with the mushroom mixture (minus the salad greens) from Sautéed Wild Mushrooms on Fresh Greens (see recipe, page 28) and a sprinkling of freshly grated Parmesan cheese, or top it with Carmelo's Summer Vegetable Stew (see recipe, page 134).

2 cups	milk	500 mL
2 cups	water	500 mL
1 tsp	salt	5 mL
1 tsp	grated lime zest	5 mL
1 cup	cornmeal	250 mL
1 cup	freshly grated Parmesan cheese	250 mL
½ cup	whipping (35%) cream	125 mL
2 tbsp	butter	25 mL
	Freshly grated Parmesan cheese (optional)	

1. In a large saucepan over high heat, combine milk, water, salt and lime zest; bring to a boil. Reduce heat to medium; very gradually whisk in cornmeal. (Don't add it too quickly or mixture will become lumpy.)

2. When mixture is bubbling, reduce heat to medium-low. Cook, stirring often, for 5 to 8 minutes or until polenta is thick and fairly smooth. Stir in Parmesan cheese, cream and butter; continue to stir until butter has melted.

3. Meanwhile, bring a medium saucepan half-filled with water to a boil over high heat. Reduce heat to medium. Spoon polenta into a heatproof bowl; place bowl over saucepan of simmering water. Cook, stirring occasionally, for 20 to 30 minutes or until polenta is very smooth and no longer feels grainy when rubbed between your finger and thumb. Serve at once with with additional Parmesan cheese.

Couscous with caramelized onions

Serves 6

Although it looks like a grain, couscous is actually a tiny pasta made from semolina and water, and is a staple of North African cuisine. Most of the couscous available in North America is the instant variety — which is perfect for entertaining since it needs almost no cooking. Look for couscous near the rice in most large supermarkets.

In Morocco, couscous is often served with the rich onion topping featured in this recipe.

Kitchen Wisdom

For a simpler couscous dish (useful when you have less time to fuss), cook 2 cups (500 mL) couscous according to the instructions on the package, using chicken stock instead of water, then stir in 2 tbsp (25 mL) chopped fresh mint, 1 tbsp (15 mL) olive oil, 1 tsp (5 mL) grated lemon zest and 1/4 tsp (1 mL) black pepper.

1 tbsp	olive oil	15 mL
1	large sweet onion (such as Spanish, Vidalia or Bermuda), halved and thinly sliced	1
1/2 cup	raisins	125 mL
1 tbsp	granulated sugar	15 mL
3	whole cloves	3
1	3-inch (7.5 cm) cinnamon stick	1
1/4 tsp	black pepper	1 mL
1/4 tsp	ground ginger	1 mL
1/4 tsp	freshly grated nutmeg	1 mL
1	package (12 oz/340 g) couscous (2 cups/500 mL)	1
	Chicken stock	
1	bay leaf	1
	Fresh mint, coriander or parsley	

1. In a large heavy saucepan, heat oil over medium-high heat. Add onion; stir to coat well. Reduce heat to low; cook, covered, for 15 minutes. Add raisins, sugar, cloves, cinnamon stick, pepper, ginger and nutmeg; cook, covered and stirring occasionally, for 30 to 40 minutes or until onion is very tender, dark brown and juicy. Discard cloves and cinnamon stick.

2. In a medium saucepan, cook couscous according to package instructions, using chicken stock instead of water. Add bay leaf to stock before boiling.

3. When couscous is done, discard bay leaf. Fluff couscous with a fork; spoon into a warm shallow serving dish. Spoon onion mixture over top. Garnish with mint; serve at once.

> ### Make Ahead
> The onion mixture can be refrigerated, covered, for up to 2 days. Reheat over medium-low heat, stirring occasionally, before serving.

Louisiana pecan rice

Serves 6

Food writer Kathleen Sloan is a huge fan of New Orleans — its food, architecture and all that jazz. It was there that she discovered this wonderful nutty-flavored rice dish.

Kitchen Wisdom

When preparing celery, don't remove individual stalks — use the whole bunch, slicing it as you need it, starting from the leafy tops. Keeping the root end intact this way helps the celery stay fresh longer.

1/3 cup	chopped pecans	75 mL
1 tbsp	canola oil or vegetable oil	15 mL
1	large onion, chopped	1
1 cup	chopped celery	250 mL
1 1/2 tsp	chili powder	7 mL
1 1/2 cups	long-grain rice	375 mL
3 cups	chicken stock or vegetable stock	750 mL
1/4 tsp	salt	1 mL
1/4 tsp	black pepper	1 mL
2 tbsp	chopped fresh parsley	25 mL

1. In a small skillet over medium-high heat, toast pecans, stirring often, for 3 to 5 minutes or until golden and fragrant. (Watch them carefully; they burn easily.) Remove from heat and allow to cool completely. Set aside 2 tbsp (25 mL) pecans for garnish. In a mini chopper or food processor, process remaining pecans until finely ground. (Don't overprocess or nuts will become oily.)

2. In a medium saucepan, heat oil over medium-high heat. Add onion, celery, chili powder and ground pecans; cook, stirring, for 3 to 5 minutes or until onion is soft but not brown. Add rice, stirring to coat with onion mixture.

3. Stir in stock, salt and pepper; bring to a boil over high heat. Reduce heat to medium-low; simmer, covered, for 20 minutes or until rice is tender and liquid is absorbed. If desired, season to taste with additional salt and pepper. Spoon into a warm serving dish; sprinkle with parsley and reserved pecans. Serve at once.

> **Make Ahead**
> Pecan rice can be refrigerated, covered, for up to 3 days. Reheat in the microwave on High for 6 to 8 minutes or in a 350°F (180°C) oven for 20 to 30 minutes.

Spiced rice and lentil pilaf

Serves 6

Readily available spices transform a simple rice and lentil dish into something quite exotic.

Kitchen Wisdom

You can turn this pilaf into a main course by stirring in cubes of leftover cooked poultry or meat (or cooked shrimp) about 10 minutes before the rice is ready.

1 tbsp	canola oil or vegetable oil	15 mL
1	onion, chopped	1
2	cloves garlic, minced	2
1 tsp	minced ginger root	5 mL
1 tsp	turmeric	5 mL
1 tsp	ground coriander	5 mL
1 tsp	ground cumin	5 mL
1/4 tsp	salt	1 mL
1/4 tsp	black pepper	1 mL
Pinch	cayenne pepper (or more to taste)	Pinch
1 cup	green lentils, rinsed and drained	250 mL
4 cups	beef stock	1 L
1 cup	long-grain rice	250 mL
2	tomatoes, chopped	2
1/4 cup	chopped fresh mint	50 mL
1/4 cup	chopped fresh coriander or parsley	50 mL

1. In a large skillet, heat oil over medium-high heat. Add onion, garlic and ginger; cook, stirring, for 3 to 5 minutes or until onion is soft but not brown. Add turmeric, coriander, cumin, salt, pepper and cayenne; cook, stirring, for 1 minute.

2. Add lentils; stir to coat with spice mixture. Stir in stock and bring to a boil over high heat. Reduce heat to medium-low; simmer, covered, for 15 minutes.

3. Add rice. Simmer, covered, for 20 minutes or until rice and lentils are tender. Stir in tomatoes, mint and coriander. If desired, season to taste with additional salt and pepper. Transfer to a warm shallow serving dish; serve at once.

> ### Make Ahead
> The pilaf can be refrigerated, covered, for up to 3 days. Reheat in the microwave on High for 6 to 8 minutes or in a 350°F (180°C) oven for 20 to 30 minutes or until piping hot.

Spanish green beans

Serves 6

These are so-called because I first enjoyed them in a small restaurant in the village of Hinojosa del Duque, north of the town of Córdoba in southern Spain. It's such a simple way of turning green beans into a special-occasion dish. The version I tried in Spain included Ibérico ham; but since this delectable cured ham is difficult to find in North America, I've substituted (with apologies to Spain) Italian prosciutto. I like to serve this dish either at room temperature as a salad, in which case I include the shrimp, or hot as a side dish without the shrimp. The choice is yours.

1½ lbs	green beans, washed and trimmed	750 g
2 tbsp	olive oil	25 mL
3 cups	sliced button mushrooms (about 8 oz/250 g)	750 mL
1	clove garlic, minced	1
8 oz	cooked salad shrimp (optional), thawed if frozen	250 g
4 oz	prosciutto, trimmed of excess fat and coarsely chopped	125 g
¼ tsp	black pepper	1 mL
Pinch	salt (optional)	Pinch

1. In a large saucepan of boiling salted water, cook beans for 6 to 8 minutes or until just tender; drain well. Keep warm.

2. In a large skillet, heat oil over medium-high heat. Add mushrooms and garlic; cook, stirring, for 3 minutes or until mushrooms are golden and tender. Stir in beans, shrimp, prosciutto and pepper. Reduce heat to medium-low; cook, stirring gently, for 2 minutes or until heated through. If desired, season to taste with salt and additional pepper. Serve at once or let cool to room temperature.

> **Make Ahead**
> Green beans can be washed, trimmed then refrigerated, wrapped in a damp tea towel and sealed in a plastic bag, for up to 24 hours.

Parsnip purée with Parmesan cheese

Serves 6

There's something so comforting about vegetable purées; perhaps they remind me of baby food!

This parsnip side dish, with its flavoring of Parmesan cheese is too sophisticated for most babies but goes beautifully with the Roast Pork Loin with Spiced Pear Stuffing (see recipe, page 104).

Unlike potatoes — which turn to glue — vegetables such as parsnips, can be processed to a beautifully smooth purée in a food processor.

Kitchen Wisdom

If your food processor has a slicing disk, use it to make short work of preparing the parsnips.

2 lbs	parsnips, peeled, trimmed and thinly sliced	1 kg
1/4 tsp	salt	1 mL
1/2 cup	freshly grated Parmesan cheese	125 mL
1/2 cup	hot milk	125 mL
2 tbsp	butter	25 mL
1/4 tsp	black pepper	1 mL
1/4 tsp	freshly grated nutmeg	1 mL
2 tbsp	chopped fresh parsley	25 mL

1. In a medium saucepan over high heat, combine parsnips with just enough cold water to cover them. Add salt; bring to a boil. Reduce heat to medium-low; simmer, covered, for 20 to 25 minutes or until parsnips are very tender. Drain well; return parsnips to saucepan and place over low heat to dry out parsnips, slightly shaking saucepan occasionally to prevent them from sticking.

2. In a food processor, combine parsnips, Parmesan cheese, milk, butter, pepper and nutmeg; process until very smooth. If desired, season to taste with additional salt, pepper and nutmeg. Spoon into a warm serving dish; sprinkle with parsley. Serve at once.

> **Make Ahead**
> Parsnip purée can be refrigerated, covered, for up to 3 days. Reheat in the microwave on High for 6 to 8 minutes or in a 350°F (180°C) oven for 20 to 30 minutes.

Tapenade-Crusted Lamb Racks (page 116) served with Arpi's Splendid Polenta (page 123) and Roasted Asparagus with Coriander Butter (page 129) *Overleaf:* Over-the-Top Tomato Salad (page 144)

Roasted asparagus with coriander butter

Serves 6

Roasting the asparagus here concentrates its flavor, while the aromatic butter provides a spicy yet subtle accent.

Kitchen Wisdom

Chervil is one of the first herbs to appear in the spring — just about the time that local asparagus arrives in our stores. It's feathery leaves look like miniature parsley and have a mild aniseed flavor.

• Baking sheet

1½ lbs	slender asparagus	750 g
2 tbsp	butter	25 mL
1 tsp	ground coriander	5 mL
	Fresh chervil sprigs or chopped fresh parsley	

1. Preheat oven to 400°F (200°C). Trim woody ends of asparagus by breaking them off where they snap naturally. Spread asparagus out more or less in a single layer on baking sheet.

2. In a small saucepan, heat butter and coriander over medium-high heat until butter melts and starts to bubble. Drizzle evenly over asparagus. Roast, turning with a spatula halfway through cooking time, for 15 to 18 minutes or until asparagus is tender. Transfer to a warm serving platter; sprinkle with chervil. Serve at once.

> **Make Ahead**
> Asparagus can be refrigerated (washed, trimmed, wrapped in a damp tea towel and sealed in a plastic bag) for up to 24 hours.

Herb-glazed Brussels sprouts

Serves 6

The problem with Brussels sprouts — and, I suspect, the main reason for their legendary unpopularity — is that they are very easily overcooked to a soggy mess. When well prepared, however, they are delicious. Here, they're boiled until just tender but still crisp, then tossed in a herb-laden dressing. Brussels sprouts served this way will convert even the most confirmed skeptic.

Kitchen Wisdom

Buy Brussels sprouts that are more or less the same size so that they cook evenly.

¼ cup	coarsely chopped fresh mint	50 mL
¼ cup	coarsely chopped fresh basil	50 mL
¼ cup	olive oil	50 mL
2 tbsp	fresh lemon juice	25 mL
1 tbsp	Dijon mustard	15 mL
¼ tsp	salt	1 mL
¼ tsp	black pepper	1 mL
2 lbs	small Brussels sprouts, stems and outer leaves trimmed (if necessary) and a slit cut in stem end of each	1 kg
	Fresh mint or basil leaves and/or grated lemon zest	

1. In a mini chopper or in a bowl and using a whisk, combine mint, basil, olive oil, lemon juice, mustard, salt and pepper; process or whisk until well combined.

2. In a saucepan of boiling salted water, cook Brussels sprouts for 3 to 5 minutes or until just tender but still a little crisp. (Check by cutting one in half.) Drain well; return to saucepan.

3. Spoon dressing over Brussels sprouts; stir gently to combine. Spoon into a warm serving dish; sprinkle with mint or basil leaves and/or lemon zest. Serve at once.

> **Make Ahead**
> Brussels sprouts can be refrigerated (washed, trimmed, wrapped in a damp tea towel and sealed in a plastic bag) for up to 24 hours.
>
> The dressing can be refrigerated, covered, for up to 24 hours. Let stand at room temperature for 30 minutes then whisk before serving.

Savoy cabbage sauté

Serves 6 to 8

I love mild-tasting, tender Savoy cabbage — the one with the frilly, pretty leaves. In this simple recipe from my good friend and fellow food writer Dana McCauley, the cabbage is accented with the exotic flavor of Chinese five-spice powder, an aromatic combination of cinnamon, cloves, fennel seeds, star anise and Szechuan peppercorns. Look for it in bulk stores or the Asian section of most large supermarkets.

For another recipe using five-spice powder, try Spiced Pear Biscuits (see recipe, page 65).

• Large deep skillet with lid *or* Dutch oven

1 tsp	canola oil or vegetable oil	5 mL
1	3 oz (75 g) piece salt pork or back bacon, cut into $1/8$-inch (3 mm) cubes	1
1	onion, halved and thinly sliced	1
2 tsp	maple syrup	10 mL
1 tsp	Chinese five-spice powder	5 mL
1	head Savoy cabbage, cored and coarsely shredded (about 12 cups/3 L)	1
$1/3$ cup	chicken stock	75 mL
1 tsp	fresh lemon juice	5 mL
$1/2$ tsp	salt	2 mL
$1/2$ tsp	black pepper	2 mL

1. In skillet or Dutch oven, heat oil over medium-high heat. Add salt pork; cook, stirring often, for 5 minutes or until well browned. Reduce heat to medium; add onion, maple syrup and Chinese five-spice powder. Cook, stirring often, for 5 minutes or until onion is soft and starts to brown.

2. Stir in cabbage and chicken stock. Cook, tightly covered and stirring occasionally, for 5 to 7 minutes or until cabbage is tender. Add lemon juice, salt and pepper; stir well. Spoon into a warm serving dish. Serve at once.

North African glazed carrots

Serves 6

This easy vegetable side dish was inspired by a carrot salad I enjoyed on a visit to North Africa some years ago. The natural sweetness of the carrots marries well with exotic spices.

All three of the spices called for here are available in most large supermarkets.

2 lbs	carrots, peeled and cut into 2- by ½-inch (5 by 1 cm) pieces	1 kg
1	clove garlic, peeled but left whole	1
½ tsp	salt	2 mL
2 tbsp	olive oil	25 mL
½ tsp	paprika	2 mL
½ tsp	ground cumin	2 mL
½ tsp	ground cinnamon	2 mL
1 tbsp	fresh lemon juice	15 mL
¼ tsp	black pepper	1 mL
1 tbsp	chopped fresh parsley	15 mL

1. In a medium saucepan over high heat, combine carrots with just enough cold water to cover them. Add garlic clove and ¼ tsp (1 mL) salt; bring to a boil. Reduce heat to medium-low; cook, covered, for 20 to 25 minutes or until carrots and garlic are tender. Drain carrots well; reserve garlic separately. Return carrots to saucepan.

2. Meanwhile, in a small skillet, heat 1 tbsp (15 mL) oil over medium-high heat. Add paprika, cumin and cinnamon; cook, stirring, for 1 minute or until fragrant. Remove from heat.

3. In a small bowl, using the back of a spoon, mash garlic until smooth. Whisk in spice mixture, remaining oil, lemon juice, pepper and remaining salt. Add mixture to carrots in saucepan; toss over low heat until well combined and carrots are piping hot. If desired, season to taste with additional salt and pepper. Spoon into a warm serving dish; sprinkle with parsley. Serve at once.

> **Make Ahead**
> The carrots can be peeled, cut into pieces then refrigerated in a bowl with enough cold water to cover them, for up to 8 hours.

Snow pea and mushroom stir-fry

Serves 6

You can use any type of mushroom for this quick stir-fry, but I think shiitakes have the best flavor and texture.

Kitchen Wisdom

If you don't have a large enough wok or skillet, a large electric skillet will work well for this stir-fry.

• Large wok or skillet

1 lb	snow peas	500 g
1 tbsp	sesame oil	15 mL
8 oz	shiitake mushrooms, stems discarded and caps sliced	250 g
1/4 cup	orange juice	50 mL
1	clove garlic, minced	1
1/4 tsp	salt	1 mL
1/4 tsp	black pepper	1 mL
Pinch	hot pepper flakes	Pinch

1. With a sharp knife, trim both ends from snow peas and, as you trim, pull away the "strings" from each side of snow peas. Cut snow peas in half crosswise.

2. Heat wok or skillet over high heat. Add oil and heat until a haze appears over the surface. Add snow peas and mushrooms; stir-fry for 2 minutes.

3. Add orange juice, garlic, salt, pepper and hot pepper flakes. Stir-fry for 1 to 2 minutes or until snow peas are tender-crisp. Serve at once.

> **Make Ahead**
> Although the stir-fry must be prepared just before serving, the vegetables can be chopped and measured, then covered and refrigerated up to 24 hours ahead.

Carmelo's summer vegetable stew

Serves 6 to 8

Versions of this vegetable stew, known as pisto, *are popular all across Spain, and it's as versatile as it is fresh-tasting. Topped with halved hard-cooked eggs,* pisto *makes a good vegetarian main course. It's also good served at room temperature as an appetizer with slices of crusty baguette. But I like it best served warm as an accompaniment to roast meats, such as Tapenade-Crusted Lamb Racks (see recipe, page 116). This recipe comes via a great cook, Carmelo Solís, from his father Carmelo Solís Sánchez of La Mancha in northwest Spain. Carmelo Jr. says he owes his love of cooking — and dedicates the recipe — to his father. Many thanks to Pilar Arce Lozano and Estefanía Navascués of Toronto's Commercial Office of Spain for translating the recipe for me.*

2 lbs	ripe tomatoes	1 kg
1 tbsp	olive oil	15 mL
1	onion, finely chopped	1
1	large red or green bell pepper, seeded and cut into $\frac{1}{2}$-inch (1 cm) pieces	1
2	medium zucchini, cut into $\frac{1}{2}$-inch (1 cm) cubes	2
$\frac{1}{2}$ tsp	salt	2 mL
$\frac{1}{4}$ tsp	black pepper	1 mL
$\frac{1}{2}$ tsp	granulated sugar	2 mL
1	egg, beaten	1
	Fresh basil sprigs	

1. Fill a large bowl with cold water. With a sharp knife, cut an "x" in the skin at the base of each tomato. In a large saucepan of boiling water, simmer tomatoes for 1 minute or until tomato skins split. With a slotted spoon, remove tomatoes from saucepan and immediately place in the bowl of cold water.

2. When tomatoes are cool enough to handle, carefully peel off skins. With a sharp knife, cut out stem ends from tomatoes; discard. Chop tomatoes coarsely; set aside.

3. In a large skillet, heat oil over medium-high heat. Add onion and pepper; cook, stirring occasionally, for 3 to 5 minutes or until onion is lightly browned. Add zucchini, salt and pepper; cook, stirring occasionally, for 3 to 5 minutes or until pepper is tender and starting to brown.

4. Add tomatoes. Reduce heat to medium-low; simmer, uncovered and stirring occasionally, for 20 to 30 minutes or until vegetables are tender and most of the liquid has evaporated.

Kitchen Wisdom

Although this is best made in late summer when local tomatoes are in season, it's almost as good prepared at other times during the year using vine-ripened hothouse tomatoes sold on the stem. Let hothouse tomatoes stand at room temperature for 3 to 5 days until the stems are dry and the tomatoes are fully ripe. Never, ever refrigerate tomatoes or their texture will become woolly.

5. Add sugar; stir well. Add egg; cook, stirring, for 2 to 3 minutes or until creamy and slightly thickened. If desired, season to taste with additional salt and pepper. Spoon into a warm serving dish; garnish with basil. Serve at once. (Alternatively, let cool and serve at room temperature, garnished with basil.)

Variations

Substitute 1 medium Italian eggplant for the zucchini.

If good-tasting ripe tomatoes are unavailable, use one 28-oz (796 mL) can diced tomatoes instead.

Make Ahead
The stew can be refrigerated, covered, for up to 3 days. Let stand at room temperature for 30 minutes before serving cold, or reheat over medium heat until piping hot.

Honey-dill asparagus and baby carrots

Serves 6

Here is a lovely spring dish to serve when local asparagus is at its best.

Kitchen Wisdom

To ritz up a simple side of carrots or peas, toss them with a little olive oil after cooking then serve sprinkled with ¼ cup (50 mL) finely chopped fresh parsley, 2 tsp (10 mL) finely grated lemon zest and 1 finely minced clove of garlic.

1 lb	asparagus	500 g
1 lb	baby carrots (thickest ones cut in half lengthwise)	500 g
¼ tsp	salt	1 mL
2 tbsp	butter	25 mL
2 tsp	honey	10 mL
3 tbsp	chopped fresh dill	45 mL

1. Trim woody ends of asparagus by breaking them off where they snap naturally. Cut asparagus into 2-inch (5 cm) pieces.

2. In a large saucepan over high heat, combine carrots with enough cold water to cover them. Add salt; bring to a boil. Reduce heat to low; simmer, covered, for 2 minutes. Increase heat to high. Add asparagus; bring to a boil. Reduce heat to low; simmer, uncovered, for 2 to 3 minutes or until asparagus and carrots are just tender. Drain well; set aside.

3. Thoroughly dry saucepan. Melt butter and honey in saucepan over medium heat. Add asparagus, carrots and dill; cook, stirring gently, for 2 to 3 minutes or until vegetables are well coated with butter mixture and are piping hot. Serve at once.

> **Make Ahead**
> Asparagus and carrots can be refrigerated (washed, trimmed, wrapped in a damp tea towel and sealed in a plastic bag) for up to 24 hours.

Salads

See also...

Spinach and watercress salad with apricots

Serves 8

This colorful salad works equally well with washed and torn romaine lettuce substituted for either the spinach or watercress.

Kitchen Wisdom

I like to serve a salad as the French do, after the main course; it tastes more refreshing that way. Also, not only is there more room on the table but, because the salad and dressing can be prepared ahead of time and tossed together at the last minute, it gives you a little breathing space between serving the main course and dessert.

The easiest way to chop dried fruits is to snip them into small pieces with sharp kitchen scissors.

½ cup	chopped walnuts	125 mL
1 cup	dried apricots, chopped	250 mL
½ cup	dry white wine	125 mL
⅓ cup	walnut oil or olive oil	75 mL
2 tbsp	white wine vinegar	25 mL
1 tsp	liquid honey	5 mL
¼ tsp	salt	1 mL
¼ tsp	black pepper	1 mL
6 cups	washed, dried and torn spinach leaves, tough stems discarded	1.5 L
6 cups	washed and dried watercress, tough stems discarded	1.5 L

1. In a small skillet over medium-high heat, toast walnuts, stirring often, for 3 to 5 minutes or until golden and fragrant. (Watch them carefully; they burn easily.) Remove from heat; let cool completely.

2. In a small bowl, stir together apricots and wine. Let stand for 1 hour, stirring occasionally. With a slotted spoon, remove apricots, reserving wine in bowl. Whisk oil, vinegar, honey, salt and pepper into wine.

3. Just before serving, combine spinach, watercress and apricots in a large salad bowl. Add dressing; toss well. Sprinkle with walnuts; serve at once.

Make Ahead
Greens can be washed, dried and torn, then wrapped loosely in paper towels and refrigerated in a sealed plastic bag for up to 2 days.

The dressing can be refrigerated, covered, for up to 1 week. Let stand at room temperature for 30 minutes and then whisk well before using.

Coleslaw with Asian dressing

Serves 6

Here is a pretty, refreshing salad with soya sauce and sesame oil adding an exotic touch to the vinaigrette. Thanks to Joyce Parslow, one of my trusty recipe testers, for sharing this recipe.

Kitchen Wisdom

Sesame oil is a vibrantly flavored oil that frequently appears in Asian recipes. It has a strong flavor so use sparingly. Look for sesame oil in the Asian section of your supermarket. It will be labeled as pure sesame oil or as a blend of sesame and soybean oils — either type is fine for this recipe.

Rice vinegar is made from fermented and soured rice wine. Look for it in the Asian section of your supermarket. If unavailable, substitute white or red wine vinegar.

To toast almonds, spread out in a small skillet; toast over medium-high heat, stirring often, for 3 to 5 minutes or until golden and fragrant. (Watch them carefully; they burn easily.) Remove from heat; let cool completely.

Dressing

½ cup	canola oil or vegetable oil	125 mL
¼ cup	rice vinegar	50 mL
1 tbsp	soya sauce	15 mL
1½ tsp	brown sugar	7 mL
1	clove garlic, minced	1
1 tsp	minced ginger root	5 mL
1 tsp	sesame oil	5 mL

Salad

1 cup	snow peas (about 3 oz/75 g)	250 mL
3 cups	shredded napa cabbage	750 mL
3 cups	shredded bok choy	750 mL
1 cup	bean sprouts	250 mL
¼ cup	chopped green onions	50 mL
½ cup	dried cranberries (optional)	125 mL
¼ cup	toasted sliced or slivered almonds	50 mL

1. **Dressing:** In a small bowl, whisk together canola oil, rice vinegar, soya sauce, brown sugar, garlic, ginger and sesame oil, until sugar is dissolved.

2. **Salad:** With a small sharp knife, trim both ends from snow peas and, as you trim, pull away the "strings" from each side of snow peas. Cut snow peas in half crosswise.

3. In a small saucepan of boiling water, cook snow peas for 2 minutes. Drain in a colander or large sieve. Rinse under cold running water; drain well.

4. In a large salad bowl, toss together snow peas, napa cabbage, bok choy, bean sprouts and green onions. Just before serving, add dressing and cranberries to salad; toss well. Sprinkle with almonds; serve at once.

> **Make Ahead**
> The dressing can be refrigerated, covered, for up to 1 week. Let stand at room temperature for 30 minutes, then whisk well before using.

The best-ever Caesar salad

Serves 4 to 6

I make no apologies for including such a well-known dish in this book because I really think this recipe is the best I've ever tasted. When it appeared in Homemaker's Magazine *some years ago, a reader who owned a restaurant in the Maritimes phoned to tell me she'd replaced the regular Caesar salad on her menu with my version — praise indeed.*

Kitchen Wisdom

For best results, use freshly squeezed lemon juice, the finest-quality olive oil and freshly grated Parmigiano-Reggiano cheese (the genuine article has its name stamped on the rind). Don't even *think* of using the so-called Parmesan that comes ready-grated in canisters. I like to grate the Parmesan using the largest holes on a cheese grater.

• Baking sheet

1	day-old 6-inch (15 cm) panini or Italian bun, cut into ½-inch (1 cm) cubes	1
3 tbsp	olive oil	45 mL
1 or 2	cloves garlic, peeled and cut in half	1 or 2
8 to 10 cups	romaine lettuce (1 head), washed, dried and torn	2 to 2.5 L

Dressing

⅓ cup	olive oil	75 mL
2	hard-cooked eggs, peeled and chopped	2
2 tbsp	fresh lemon juice	25 mL
2 tsp	anchovy paste or ¼ tsp (1 mL) salt	10 mL
1 tsp	Worcestershire sauce	5 mL
¼ tsp	black pepper	1 mL
½ cup	freshly grated Parmesan cheese	125 mL

1. Preheat oven to 350°F (180°C). Spread bread cubes out on baking sheet. Bake for 5 minutes or until crisp but not colored. In a bowl, combine bread cubes and oil; toss gently to coat. Place cubes back on baking sheet. Bake for 3 to 5 minutes or until golden. Set aside to cool completely.

2. Rub cut sides of garlic around inside of large salad bowl; reserve garlic for dressing. Place lettuce in bowl; refrigerate, covered, until ready to serve.

Kitchen Wisdom

To hard-cook eggs, place them in a small saucepan and cover with cold water. Bring to a boil, then reduce heat to medium-low and simmer, uncovered, for 7 to 8 minutes. Drain well in a colander, then let stand under cold running water until cool enough to handle. Tap eggs gently on counter to crack shells before peeling them.

3. **Dressing:** Slice reserved garlic. In a food processor or blender, combine garlic, oil, eggs, lemon juice, anchovy paste, Worcestershire sauce and pepper; process until fairly smooth, scraping down sides of processor once or twice.

4. Just before serving, add dressing, croutons and cheese to lettuce; toss well. Serve in chilled salad bowls. If desired, serve additional black pepper and grated Parmesan cheese at the table.

> ### Make Ahead
> Croutons can be stored in an airtight container for up to 5 days.
>
> The dressing can be refrigerated, covered, for up to 3 days. Let stand at room temperature for 30 minutes; whisk well before using.
>
> Romaine lettuce can be washed, dried and torn, then wrapped loosely in paper towels and refrigerated in a sealed plastic bag for up to 2 days.

Arugula and Boston lettuce with sherry vinaigrette and pine nuts

Serves 6

I absolutely adore arugula. Its slightly bitter, almost aromatic flavor means it needs very little embellishment. Here, the leaves are combined with tender Boston lettuce and simply tossed with a garlicky dressing and some pine nuts.

Serve this salad after a robust main course, such as Pot Roast of Beef with Wild Mushrooms (see recipe, page 98) or Seafood Pot Pie with Rösti Topping (see recipe, page 72).

Kitchen Wisdom

If you can't find arugula, kick up a fuss with the manager of your supermarket. In the meantime, substitute watercress (with its thicker stems discarded).

Sherry vinegar is available at some supermarkets but if you can't find it, substitute a good-quality balsamic vinegar.

½ cup	pine nuts	125 mL
4 cups	washed, dried and torn arugula	1 L
4 cups	washed, dried and torn Boston lettuce	1 L
⅓ cup	olive oil	75 mL
2 tbsp	sherry vinegar or balsamic vinegar	25 mL
2	cloves garlic, minced	2
1	shallot, finely minced	1
¼ tsp	salt	1 mL
¼ tsp	black pepper	1 mL

1. In a small skillet over medium-high heat, toast pine nuts, stirring often, for 3 to 5 minutes or until golden and fragrant. (Watch carefully; they burn easily.) Remove from heat; let cool completely.

2. Place arugula and Boston lettuce in a large salad bowl; refrigerate, covered, until ready to serve.

3. In a small jar with a lid, combine olive oil, vinegar, garlic, shallot, salt and pepper; shake until well mixed.

4. Just before serving, add dressing to greens; toss well. Sprinkle with pine nuts. Serve at once.

Make Ahead
The greens can be washed, dried and torn, then wrapped loosely in paper towels and refrigerated in a sealed plastic bag for up to 2 days.

The dressing can be refrigerated for up to 1 week. Let stand at room temperature for 30 minutes, then shake well before using.

White bean salad with lemon-dill vinaigrette

Serves 6 to 8

Bean salads can be so disappointing. But this one is fresh-tasting and holds up well for several hours without refrigeration — perfect for a buffet table.

Kitchen Wisdom

Dill is one of the few fresh herbs that freeze well. Simply place in a plastic bag and freeze for up to 6 months. To use, just break off what you need from the frozen bunch. For best results, add to cooked dishes rather than salads.

2	cans (each 19 oz/540 mL) white kidney beans, rinsed and drained	2
2	small tomatoes, chopped	2
½ cup	finely chopped red onion	125 mL
¼ cup	chopped fresh dill	50 mL
¼ cup	olive oil	50 mL
2 tbsp	fresh lemon juice	25 mL
1 tbsp	liquid honey	15 mL
¼ tsp	salt	1 mL
¼ tsp	black pepper	1 mL

1. In a large serving bowl, combine beans, tomatoes, onion and 3 tbsp (45 mL) dill.

2. In a small bowl, whisk together olive oil, lemon juice, honey, salt and pepper. Add to beans; toss well. If desired, season to taste with additional salt and pepper. Serve garnished with remaining dill.

> **Make Ahead**
> The bean salad can be refrigerated for up to 8 hours. Let stand at room temperature for 30 minutes before serving.

Over-the-top tomato salad

Serves 6

In this attractive salad, fresh tomatoes are drizzled with a vibrant sun-dried tomato dressing.

Kitchen Wisdom

If you use sun-dried tomatoes packed in oil, there's no need to soak them and you can use their oil in place of the olive oil.

The easiest way to chop sun-dried tomatoes is to snip them into small pieces with sharp kitchen scissors.

Wrap leftover red onion tightly in plastic wrap and refrigerate for up to 1 week.

2 tbsp	coarsely chopped sun-dried tomatoes	25 mL
	Boiling water	
2 tbsp	olive oil	25 mL
1 tbsp	chopped red onion	15 mL
1 tbsp	balsamic vinegar	15 mL
1/4 tsp	granulated sugar	1 mL
1/4 tsp	salt	1 mL
1/4 tsp	black pepper	1 mL
3	beefsteak tomatoes (each about 8 oz/250 g)	3
1/4 cup	small fresh basil or oregano leaves	50 mL

1. In a small heatproof bowl, combine sun-dried tomatoes with enough boiling water to cover them; set aside for 20 minutes. Drain tomatoes well, reserving water.

2. In a blender or mini-chopper, combine sun-dried tomatoes, 2 tbsp (25 mL) reserved soaking water (use tap water if using oil-packed sun-dried tomatoes), oil, onion, vinegar, sugar, salt and pepper. Blend until finely minced and well combined. (Dressing will be quite thick.)

3. With a small knife, cut out coarse stem ends from beefsteak tomatoes. Cut tomatoes into thin slices; arrange on a serving platter. Just before serving, whisk dressing to combine; spoon evenly over tomatoes. Serve sprinkled with basil leaves.

> **Make Ahead**
> The dressing can be refrigerated, covered, for up to 1 week. Let stand at room temperature for 30 minutes, then whisk well before using.

Potato and snow-pea salad with mint-pesto dressing

Serves 6

Pine nuts add authentic pesto texture to this pungent dressing, but they can be omitted if one of your guests has a nut allergy.

Kitchen Wisdom

To toast pine nuts, spread them out in a small skillet; toast over medium-high heat, stirring often, for 3 to 5 minutes, or until golden and fragrant. (Watch carefully; they burn easily.) Remove from heat; let cool completely.

2½ cups	snow peas (about 8 oz/250 g)	625 mL
1¾ lbs	small new potatoes, scrubbed	875 g

Mint-Pesto Dressing

½ cup	loosely packed fresh mint leaves	125 mL
¼ cup	snipped fresh chives	50 mL
¼ cup	olive oil	50 mL
2 tbsp	toasted pine nuts	25 mL
2 tbsp	freshly grated Parmesan cheese	25 mL
¼ tsp	salt	1 mL
¼ tsp	black pepper	1 mL

1. With a small sharp knife, trim both ends from snow peas and, as you trim, pull away the "strings" from each side of snow peas. In a large saucepan of boiling salted water, cook snow peas for 2 to 3 minutes or until just tender. With a slotted spoon, remove snow peas to a colander or large sieve. Rinse under cold running water; drain well.

2. In same saucepan of boiling salted water, cook potatoes for 15 to 20 minutes or until just tender. Drain well; return potatoes to saucepan. Place over low heat to dry out potatoes slightly. Remove from heat. When cool enough to handle, cut any large potatoes in half. In a large salad bowl, gently stir together potatoes and snow peas.

3. **Mint-Pesto Dressing:** In a mini-chopper or food processor, combine mint, 3 tbsp (45 mL) chives, oil, pine nuts, Parmesan cheese, salt and pepper; process until fairly smooth. Add dressing to potatoes and snow peas; toss gently. Serve at once, sprinkled with remaining chives.

Escarole salad with olives

I enjoyed a salad very much like this one at a country inn located in the rolling hills of Navarra in northern Spain. There, it was made with a baby lettuce called cogollo, *very much like frilly-leafed escarole, which is easier to find in North America.*

If you prefer, omit the anchovies — but their robust flavor adds an interesting dimension to this salad.

Kitchen Wisdom

Always store cans of anchovies, whether opened or not, in the refrigerator. Once opened, pat the anchovies dry with paper towels. Leftovers can be frozen, wrapped in plastic wrap, for up to 1 month.

8 cups	washed, dried and torn escarole	2 L
⅔ cup	olive oil	150 mL
¼ cup	red wine vinegar	50 mL
1	clove garlic, minced	1
½ tsp	black pepper	2 mL
½ cup	chopped fresh parsley	125 mL
1	can (2 oz/50 g) anchovies, drained and coarsely chopped	1
½ cup	pitted black olives	125 mL
½ cup	pitted green olives	125 mL

1. Place escarole in a large salad bowl; refrigerate, covered, until ready to serve.

2. In a small jar with a lid, combine olive oil, vinegar, garlic and pepper; shake until well mixed.

3. Just before serving, add dressing and parsley to escarole; toss well. Scatter anchovies, black olives and green olives over top. Serve at once.

> ## Make Ahead
> Escarole can be washed, dried and torn, then wrapped loosely in paper towels and refrigerated in a sealed plastic bag for up to 2 days.
>
> The dressing can be refrigerated for up to 1 week. Let stand at room temperature for 30 minutes, then shake well before using.

Desserts

Cherry-cinnamon bread-and-butter pudding

Serves 6 to 8

Replacing the more usual slices of bread with buttery croissants makes this simple dessert positively ambrosial; it's light yet rich, but not too sweet. Serve it to your guests, along with scoops of vanilla ice cream or dollops of softly whipped cream, and they'll be your friends for life.

Kitchen Wisdom

A miniature bottle of brandy or rum (airline size) contains the 1/4 cup (50 mL) needed for this recipe.

Before grating zest from oranges, wash them in warm soapy water, then rinse and dry well. This removes any waxy coating from the oranges.

To squeeze as much juice as possible from oranges, roll them on the counter with the palm of your hand before cutting them in half.

A citrus zester is one of my favorite gadgets and is invaluable for scraping every last vestige of colored zest from citrus fruit.

Store whole citrus fruit in the fridge after grating zest. Although the remaining rind will dry out, the fruit can be used for juice for up to 1 week.

• Preheat broiler
• 11- by 7-inch (2 L) baking dish, lightly buttered

1 cup	dried cherries (about 4 oz/125 g)	250 mL
1/4 cup	brandy or dark or amber rum or orange juice	50 mL
1/4 cup	packed brown sugar	50 mL
1 tsp	grated orange zest	5 mL
1/2 tsp	ground cinnamon	2 mL
4	day-old croissants, cut in half horizontally	4
1/4 cup	butter, softened	50 mL
2 cups	homogenized (whole) milk	500 mL
3	eggs	3

1. In a small bowl, stir together cherries and brandy; let stand for 30 minutes. In another small bowl, combine brown sugar, orange zest and cinnamon; set aside.

2. Place croissants, cut-side up, under hot broiler about 4 inches (10 cm) from heat. Broil for 1 minute or until lightly toasted. Spread butter on cut side of each croissant, dividing evenly. Arrange 4 of the croissant halves butter-side down in baking dish, overlapping slightly if necessary.

3. Drain cherries, reserving brandy. Sprinkle cherries and half brown-sugar mixture over croissants. Arrange remaining croissant halves, butter-side up, on top of cherries. Sprinkle with remaining brown-sugar mixture.

4. In a 4-cup (1 L) liquid measure, whisk together milk, eggs and reserved brandy. Strain mixture through a sieve into baking dish, drizzling evenly over croissants. Let stand for 30 minutes, occasionally pressing croissants down to ensure they are well soaked.

5. Meanwhile, preheat oven to 350°F (180°C). Bake, uncovered, for 40 to 50 minutes or until puffy, golden brown and crisp. Serve at once.

Peppered strawberry-mascarpone ice cream

Serves 4 to 6
Makes 4 cups (1 L)

This may be the easiest ice cream in the world and it's a great way to use up overripe fruit. The combination of strawberries and black pepper may surprise you, but the flavors go perfectly. Try grinding a little black pepper over your next bowl of strawberries and cream. Trust me; it's delicious!

Kitchen Wisdom

Mascarpone cheese is a very rich, thick Italian cream cheese; look for it in the deli cheese section of your supermarket.

If you are short of time or don't have an ice-cream maker, simply spoon ice cream into serving dishes and freeze for 1 hour before serving. The dessert will be softly frozen and just as delicious.

5 cups	hulled sliced strawberries (about 1 quart/1 L whole berries)	1.25 L
1 cup	icing sugar, sifted	250 mL
8 oz	mascarpone cheese	250 g
1 tsp	freshly ground black pepper	5 mL

1. In a food processor, combine strawberries and icing sugar; process until fairly smooth. Add mascarpone and pepper; process until ingredients are well combined.

2. Spoon strawberry mixture into an ice-cream maker; churn according to manufacturer's instructions. Serve at once or spoon into a lidded container and store in the freezer.

3. Alternatively, if you don't have an ice-cream maker, spoon strawberry mixture into a shallow freezerproof container and freeze until there is a 1-inch (2.5 cm) frozen border around the edge. Scrape partially frozen ice cream into a bowl; beat with an electric mixer at high speed until smooth. Repeat this freezing and beating process twice more, then freeze until firm.

> **Make Ahead**
> Ice cream can be frozen for up to 1 week (any longer and it loses its fresh taste). Transfer ice cream to the refrigerator for 30 minutes to soften before serving.

Chocolate-fudge pie with orange compote

Serves 10 to 12

My sister Lucy — a chocoholic if ever there was one — concocted this simple but decadent chocolate dessert; I added the fresh-tasting orange compote. If you prefer, serve the pie with fresh berries and/or softly whipped cream instead of the compote. Use a good quality eating (not baking) chocolate for this dessert — one with at least 70% cocoa solids in it (check the label). For adults, add Grand Marnier or other orange-flavored liqueur; for children, replace the liqueur with orange juice.

- 9-inch (2.5 L) or 10-inch (3 L) springform pan

1	package (11 oz/350 g) chocolate-fudge sandwich cookies (about 26), broken into pieces	1
¼ cup	butter, melted	50 mL
12 oz	good-quality semi-sweet chocolate	375 g
2 tbsp	corn syrup	25 mL
2 cups	whipping (35%) cream	500 mL
¼ cup	Grand Marnier or orange juice	50 mL
1 tbsp	finely grated orange zest	15 mL

Orange Compote

8	oranges	8
¼ cup	granulated sugar	50 mL
1	3-inch (7.5 cm) cinnamon stick	1
2 tbsp	Grand Marnier (optional)	25 mL

1. In a food processor, combine cookies and butter; process using on-off pulses until cookies are reduced to fine crumbs and mixture is well combined. Spread cookie mixture out over base of springform pan, pressing down with back of a spoon. Set aside.

2. In the top half of a double boiler or in a heatproof bowl standing over a saucepan of hot (not boiling) water, melt chocolate with corn syrup and ¼ cup (50 mL) whipping cream; stir until mixture is smooth. Remove from heat; stir in Grand Marnier. Let cool until mixture is lukewarm.

3. Place a medium bowl and the beaters of electric mixer in the freezer; chill for 15 minutes. Pour remaining cream into chilled bowl; beat with electric mixer at high speed until it holds soft peaks. With a large spoon or rubber spatula, using a gentle cutting motion, fold one-quarter of the whipped cream into the chocolate mixture to lighten it. Spoon chocolate mixture into remaining whipped cream and fold in until no white streaks remain.

A miniature bottle of Grand Marnier (airline size) contains $\frac{1}{4}$ cup (50 mL).

For a mocha-flavored version, substitute $\frac{1}{4}$ cup (50 mL) strong black coffee for the Grand Marnier or orange juice. Serve with softly whipped cream instead of the orange compote.

4. Pour chocolate mixture over prepared crust. Refrigerate, tightly covered, for at least 8 hours or overnight. Remove pie from refrigerator. Release sides of pan; slide dessert onto a serving plate. Scatter orange zest over surface of pie; serve with orange compote.

5. **Orange Compote:** With a small sharp knife, cut a slice from end of 1 orange. Holding the orange over a bowl to catch juice, cut away zest and white pith. Holding peeled orange in the palm of your hand, cut between membranes to release each orange segment; place segments in a shallow serving bowl. Repeat with remaining oranges.

6. Pour $\frac{1}{2}$ cup (125 mL) reserved orange juice into a small saucepan. Add sugar and cinnamon stick; bring to a boil over high heat. Reduce heat to medium-low; simmer for 2 minutes. Pour juice mixture over orange segments; stir in Grand Marnier. Let cool completely. Discard cinnamon stick before serving.

> **Make Ahead**
> The pie must be refrigerated for at least 8 hours or up to 24 hours before serving.

Exotic fruit salad

Serves 8 to 10

Crunchy edible pomegranate seeds add a splash of festive red color to this refreshing fruit salad, but if serving the salad to very young children, omit the pomegranate (the small seeds could cause them to choke). Leave out the Grand Marnier if you like or simply add it to the salad after serving the children.

2	papayas	2
2	mangoes	2
1	pomegranate	1
4	kiwi fruit, peeled, cut in half lengthwise and sliced	4
1	pineapple, peeled, cored and cut into $\frac{1}{2}$-inch (1 cm) cubes	1
	Grated zest of 1 orange	
	Freshly squeezed juice of 1 orange	
	Grated zest of 1 lime	
	Freshly squeezed juice of 1 lime	
2 tbsp	liquid honey	25 mL
2 tbsp	Grand Marnier (optional)	25 mL

1. Cut papayas in half; scoop out and discard seeds. Cut papayas lengthwise into wedges. Cut fruit from skin; cut into $\frac{1}{2}$-inch (1 cm) cubes.

2. Place one mango on counter with its narrowest side uppermost. With a large sharp knife, slice down through mango, cutting each side away from pit and slicing as close to the pit as possible. With the point of a knife, cut a crosshatch pattern in the flesh of the two pieces you have cut off. Turn slices "inside out;" cut cubes of mango flesh away from skin. Cut the skin from the mango that remains around pit; cut any remaining mango flesh from pit. Repeat with remaining mango.

3. With a large sharp knife, cut a slice from top of pomegranate. Score skin of pomegranate, dividing fruit into quarters. Break fruit apart; with your fingers, remove the small flesh-covered seeds, discarding any of the yellowish-white membrane.

Kitchen Wisdom

According to legend, it was a pomegranate, not an apple, with which Eve tempted Adam in the Garden of Eden. And no wonder — beneath its hard leathery skin, the pomegranate contains small edible seeds surrounded by wonderfully sweet glossy pink flesh. The seeds can be added to fruit salads or used as a garnish for other desserts; the flesh is used to make grenadine, a popular ingredient in cocktails.

4. In a large glass serving bowl, combine papayas, mangoes, pomegranate, kiwi and pineapple; stir gently.

5. In a small bowl, whisk together orange zest, orange juice, lime zest, lime juice, honey and Grand Marnier. Pour juice mixture over fruit; stir gently. Let stand at room temperature for 1 hour to allow flavors to blend.

Variation

If you prefer, remove the skin and seeds of 1 medium cantaloupe, cut flesh into $1/2$-inch (1 cm) cubes and use in place of the papayas and mangoes.

Make Ahead
The fruit salad can be refrigerated for up to 8 hours. Let stand at room temperature for 30 minutes before serving, then stir gently.

Thanksgiving crème brûlées

Serves 8

The mildly spiced flavor of these rich crème brûlées echoes the taste of old-fashioned pumpkin pie, but that doesn't mean you can't serve this decadent treat at other times of the year.

- Eight ½-cup (125 mL) ramekins
- Shallow baking pan just large enough to hold ramekins

2 cups	whipping (35%) cream	500 mL
1 cup	homogenized (whole) milk	250 mL
1	3-inch (7.5 cm) cinnamon stick	1
4	whole cloves	4
¼ tsp	ground allspice	1 mL
¼ tsp	freshly grated nutmeg	1 mL
6	egg yolks	6
¼ cup	granulated sugar	50 mL
1 tsp	vanilla	5 mL
½ cup	packed brown sugar	125 mL

1. Preheat oven to 325°F (160°C). In a saucepan over medium heat, stir together cream, milk, cinnamon stick, cloves, allspice and nutmeg. Heat for 5 to 7 minutes or until mixture is steaming and bubbles appear around the edge. Remove from heat; let stand, covered, for 10 minutes.

2. In a medium bowl, combine egg yolks, granulated sugar and vanilla; beat just until combined. Strain cream mixture through a fine sieve into a pitcher; discard cinnamon stick and cloves. Gradually whisk strained cream mixture into egg-yolk mixture.

3. Using a ladle, divide mixture evenly among ramekins. Place ramekins in baking pan. Pour hot water into baking pan to come halfway up sides of ramekins. Bake for 30 to 35 minutes or until cream mixture is just set but centers still wobble slightly. Remove ramekins from the oven; let cool completely. Cover each ramekin with plastic wrap; refrigerate for at least 2 hours or up to 24 hours.

4. At least 2 hours — but no more than 4 hours — before serving, sprinkle brown sugar evenly over cream mixture in each ramekin. Place ramekins on a baking sheet; place under a hot broiler for 3 to 5 minutes or until sugar melts and caramelizes. Allow to cool slightly, then refrigerate, uncovered, for at least 2 hours or up to 4 hours before serving.

Variation

Spoon 1 to 2 tbsp (15 to 25 mL) fresh wild blueberries into each ramekin before adding the strained cream mixture.

Make Ahead
Crème brûlées, without their sugar topping, can be refrigerated, covered, for up to 24 hours. Once the sugar topping is added, crème brûlées must be served within 4 hours of broiling.

Chocolate terrine with drunken pineapple

Serves 8 to 10

For best results, use good-quality eating (not baking) chocolate for this decadent make-ahead terrine.

Kitchen Wisdom

A miniature bottle of rum or brandy (airline size) contains the ¼ cup (50 mL) needed for this recipe.

• 8- by 4-inch (1.5 L) loaf pan

1	can (14 oz/398 mL) pineapple tidbits in juice, well drained and patted dry with paper towels	1
¼ cup	dark or amber rum or brandy	50 mL
1 tsp	vanilla	5 mL
8 oz	good-quality semi-sweet or bittersweet chocolate, coarsely chopped	250 g
⅓ cup	butter, cut into pieces	75 mL
¾ cup	half-and-half (10%) cream	175 mL
12 oz	2-inch (5 cm) gingersnap cookies (about 42)	375 g
	Softly whipped cream	
	Fresh mint sprigs	
	Fresh fruit (such as raspberries, blueberries, strawberries or grapes)	
	Unsweetened cocoa powder	

1. In a large bowl, stir together pineapple, rum and vanilla. Let stand for 1 hour, stirring occasionally.

2. Use 2 pieces of plastic wrap to line base and all 4 sides of loaf pan, letting wrap hang over sides of pan by about 2 inches (5 cm). Set aside.

3. In the top half of a double boiler or in a heatproof bowl standing over a saucepan of hot (not boiling) water, melt chocolate with butter; stir until smooth. Remove from heat and let cool until mixture is lukewarm. Whisk in cream until smooth.

If serving this dessert to children, substitute $\frac{1}{4}$ cup (50 mL) juice from can of pineapple for the rum or brandy, then proceed directly to Step 2.

4. Place cookies in a large plastic bag; crush with a rolling pin or meat mallet until cookies are in $\frac{1}{2}$-inch (1 cm) pieces not crumbs. (You should have about $3\frac{1}{2}$ cups/ 875 mL cookie pieces.) Stir cookies into pineapple mixture. Add chocolate mixture; stir until ingredients are well combined.

5. Spoon mixture into prepared pan, pressing down well and smoothing top with the back of a spoon. Fold overhanging plastic wrap over terrine to cover it completely. Refrigerate for at least 6 hours or up to 24 hours, until firm.

6. To serve, unmold terrine onto a cutting board; peel off plastic wrap. With a serrated knife and using a sawing motion, cut terrine into $\frac{3}{4}$-inch (2 cm) slices, wiping knife with a damp cloth after cutting each slice. Center a slice of terrine on its side on each individual dessert plate. Garnish each slice with a dollop of whipped cream, a mint sprig and some fresh fruit; sift cocoa around edge of each plate.

Make Ahead
Terrine must be chilled for at least 6 hours, but can be refrigerated for up to 24 hours.

Pears poached in spiced red wine

Pears and cheese are natural partners (there are few things more heavenly than a ripe pear eaten with a piece of creamy gorgonzola), so try serving these pretty poached pears with chunks of Parmesan cheese. If this seems too bizarre, dollops of softly whipped cream are a lovely accompaniment too.

1	orange	1
1 cup	water	250 mL
2/3 cup	granulated sugar	150 mL
3	bay leaves	3
6	firm ripe pears, with stems	6
2 cups	full-bodied red wine, such as Cabernet Sauvignon (or more if needed)	500 mL
	Orange zest, cut into thin strips	

1. With a sharp knife, cut two 2-inch (5 cm) strips of zest from orange, avoiding white pith. Squeeze juice from orange into a saucepan just large enough to hold pears standing side by side on their wide ends. Add orange zest, water, sugar and bay leaves; heat, stirring occasionally, over medium heat until sugar dissolves.

2. With a melon baller or small teaspoon, remove cores from pears by hollowing them out from their wide ends. Peel pears, leaving stems intact. If necessary, cut a small slice from wide end of each pear so it stands upright.

3. Stand pears in orange mixture in saucepan; pour in enough wine to cover pears. If they float, place a small saucer directly on top of pears and weigh it down with a small heavy can. Bring to a boil over medium-high heat. Reduce heat to low; cook, covered, for 15 to 30 minutes or until pears are tender but not broken up. (The time will vary depending on size and ripeness of pears, so check every 10 minutes.)

Don't use overripe pears for this recipe or they may disintegrate during poaching. On the other hand, if pears are not quite ripe, store them in a brown paper bag for 1 to 2 days until ripe and fragrant.

4. With a slotted spoon, remove pears from poaching liquid; drain well, reserving poaching liquid in saucepan. Arrange pears upright in a deep serving dish. Set aside. Over high heat, bring poaching liquid to a boil; boil, stirring occasionally, for 20 to 25 minutes or until it is reduced to about 1 cup (250 mL) and forms a syrupy sauce. Watch carefully towards end of cooking time to make sure sauce doesn't scorch.

5. Strain sauce through a sieve into a small pitcher, discarding orange zest and bay leaves. Spoon sauce over pears; let cool completely, basting pears occasionally with sauce as they cool.

6. To serve, spoon some sauce onto each of 6 dessert plates. Place a pear on each plate; drizzle with remaining sauce. Serve garnished with orange zest.

> ### Make Ahead
> Poached pears in sauce can be refrigerated, covered, for 24 hours; let stand at room temperature for 1 hour before serving.

Pumpkin ice cream pie

Serves 10 to 12

This fun alternative to traditional pumpkin pie can be prepared up to 1 week ahead. Remember to remove the pie from the freezer up to 1 hour before serving to give it time to soften slightly.

Kitchen Wisdom

Make sure you buy pumpkin purée — not pie filling — for this recipe; pumpkin purée is unsweetened and has no other flavorings added.

Make Ahead

Pie must be frozen for at least 8 hours, or can be frozen for up to 1 week.

- 10-inch (3 L) springform pan

½ cup	chopped walnuts	125 mL
3 cups	graham-wafer crumbs (about 32 cookies)	750 mL
¼ cup	granulated sugar	50 mL
½ cup	butter, melted	125 mL
6 cups	softened vanilla ice cream	1.5 L
1	can (14 oz/398 mL) pumpkin purée (not pie filling)	1
¼ cup	liquid honey	50 mL
1 tsp	pumpkin-pie spice	5 mL

1. In a small skillet over medium-high heat, toast walnuts, stirring often, for 3 to 5 minutes or until golden and fragrant. (Watch carefully; they burn easily.) Remove from heat; let cool completely.

2. In a large bowl, stir together walnuts, graham-wafer crumbs and sugar. Add butter; stir until well combined. Measure out 1 cup (250 mL) crumb mixture and set aside. Press remaining crumb mixture over base of springform pan.

3. In another large bowl, combine ice cream, pumpkin purée, honey and pumpkin-pie spice; whisk until smooth and creamy. Pour ice-cream mixture over crumb base. Sprinkle evenly with reserved crumb mixture. Cover pan tightly with plastic wrap; freeze for about 8 hours or until firm.

4. To serve, let pie stand at room temperature for 30 minutes to 1 hour to soften slightly. Release sides of pan and slide pie onto a serving plate. Cut into wedges and serve.

Pears Poached in Spiced Red Wine (page 158)

Peach and blueberry streusel tart

Serves 6

When peaches and blueberries are in season, team them together in this easy pie. At other times of the year, substitute frozen fruit, thawed and patted dry.

Kitchen Wisdom

Veteran Canadian food writer Iris Raven once said to me, "If you aren't a good baker, it makes no more sense to make your own pastry than to churn your own butter." Sage advice indeed, so don't worry about using frozen pastry if baking is not your forte.

Make Ahead

If you don't plan to serve this pie warm, it can be refrigerated, covered, for up to 24 hours; let stand at room temperature for 30 minutes before serving.

- Baking sheet

1	frozen 9-inch (22.5 cm) deep-dish pie shell	1
1	can (5 oz/160 mL) evaporated milk	1
1	egg	1
3 tbsp	packed brown sugar	45 mL
2 tbsp	all-purpose flour	25 mL
½ tsp	ground cinnamon	2 mL
2 cups	sliced pitted peaches (about 3)	500 mL
1 cup	blueberries (preferably wild)	250 mL

Streusel Topping

½ cup	packed brown sugar	125 mL
½ cup	all-purpose flour	125 mL
¼ cup	cold butter, cut into pieces	50 mL
	Vanilla ice cream	

1. Preheat oven to 425°F (220°C). Put pastry-lined pie plate on baking sheet; set aside.

2. In a medium bowl, whisk together milk, egg, sugar, flour and cinnamon until mixture is smooth. Stir in peaches and blueberries. Pour mixture into pie shell.

3. **Streusel Topping:** In a mini-chopper or food processor, combine sugar, flour and butter; process until mixture resembles coarse crumbs. (Alternatively, in a bowl, stir together sugar and flour; with a pastry blender or 2 knives, cut in butter until mixture resembles coarse crumbs.) Sprinkle mixture evenly over pie.

4. Bake for 10 minutes. Reduce temperature to 350°F (180°C); bake for 35 minutes or until tart is golden brown and filling is bubbly. Serve warm or at room temperature, with vanilla ice cream.

Viennese Chocolate Triangle Cake (page 168)

Double chocolate cakes with raspberry sauce

Serves 8

These individual chocolate cakes are incredibly easy to make but look very professional. The chunk of chocolate placed on each one before baking sinks down through the cake to form a melted chocolate heart when the cakes are turned out of their dishes.

- Eight ¾-cup (175 mL) custard cups, generously sprayed with butter-flavored baking spray
- Baking sheet

Cakes

1⅓ cups	all-purpose flour	325 mL
½ cup	unsweetened cocoa powder	125 mL
1 tsp	baking soda	5 mL
½ tsp	salt	2 mL
1¼ cups	granulated sugar	300 mL
½ cup	butter, softened	125 mL
2	eggs	2
1 tsp	vanilla	5 mL
1 tbsp	fresh lemon juice or white vinegar	15 mL
	Milk	
2 oz	good-quality semi-sweet chocolate, cut into 8 equal pieces	50 g
	Icing sugar	
	Mint leaves	
	Softly whipped cream	

Raspberry Sauce

2	packages (each 10 oz/300 g) frozen unsweetened raspberries, thawed	2
2 tbsp	icing sugar	25 mL
1 tsp	fresh lemon juice	5 mL

1. **Cakes:** Preheat oven to 350°F (180°C). Measure flour, cocoa, baking soda and salt into a sieve standing over a medium bowl. Shake ingredients through sieve to combine, pressing any lumps of cocoa through sieve. Stir gently to combine.

2. In another bowl, with an electric mixer on high speed, beat sugar and butter until light and fluffy. Beat in eggs one at a time, beating well after each addition. Beat in vanilla.

For some strange reason, these decadent cakes unmold tidily only if you use baking spray to grease the custard cups, so don't be tempted to use butter instead.

The raspberry sauce is equally good served with Creamy Lemon Tart (see recipe, page 172).

3. Pour lemon juice into a 1-cup (250 mL) liquid measure; add enough milk to yield 1 cup (250 mL). Gently stir flour mixture into sugar mixture in 4 additions, adding one-quarter of milk mixture each time, until ingredients are well combined and batter is smooth.

4. Divide batter evenly among custard cups, filling each two-thirds full. Top with piece of chocolate, but don't push chocolate down into batter. Bake for 25 to 30 minutes or until tops of cakes spring back when pressed lightly (centers may still be soft) and cakes are starting to pull away from sides of cups. Remove from oven; let stand for 5 minutes.

5. Trim tops of cakes to flatten them. Run a knife around edge of cups to loosen cakes. Carefully unmold cakes onto individual plates, trimmed-side down. (If any chocolate sticks to bottom of cups, carefully scrape it out and spoon onto tops of cakes.) Spoon about 2 tbsp (25 mL) raspberry sauce around each cake; dust tops of cakes with a little icing sugar. Garnish with mint. Serve with whipped cream.

6. Raspberry Sauce: Strain raspberries, reserving juice. Rub raspberries through a fine sieve into a bowl; discard seeds in sieve. Whisk icing sugar into raspberries, along with enough reserved juice to make a pouring consistency. Stir in lemon juice.

Make Ahead
Cakes can be baked, cooled, then wrapped and refrigerated for up to 24 hours. Unwrap and reheat in the microwave on High for 1 to 2 minutes per cake before serving.

Raspberry sauce can be refrigerated, covered, for up to 3 days.

Blackberry-peach ruffle pie

Serves 8

This free-form pie, with its easy make-in-the-food-processor pastry, is a cinch to prepare. Increase the number of peaches if blackberries are scarce.

• 12-inch (30 cm) round pizza pan, lightly greased

Pastry

2 cups	sifted cake-and-pastry flour	500 mL
⅔ cup	cold butter, cut into pieces	150 mL
1	egg, separated	1
2 to 3 tbsp	cold water	25 to 45 mL

Filling

3 cups	blackberries (about 1 lb/500 g)	750 mL
2 cups	sliced pitted peaches (about 3)	500 mL
¾ cup	granulated sugar	175 mL
¼ cup	all-purpose flour	50 mL
1 tsp	grated lemon zest	5 mL
½ tsp	ground cinnamon	2 mL
¼ tsp	freshly grated nutmeg	1 mL
Pinch	salt	Pinch
	Granulated sugar	
	Softly whipped cream	
	Sprigs of fresh mint	

1. **Pastry:** Preheat oven to 375°F (190°C). In a food processor, combine flour and butter; process with on-off pulses until well combined and mixture resembles coarse crumbs. In a small bowl, beat together egg yolk (reserve egg white) and 2 tbsp (25 mL) water. With motor running, add egg-yolk mixture to food processor; process just until mixture holds together, adding up to 1 tbsp (15 mL) water if necessary.

2. Turn dough out onto a lightly floured surface; knead lightly. Gather dough into a ball. Wrap in plastic wrap; refrigerate for 20 minutes.

The easiest way to separate the white and yolk of an egg is to break the egg onto a saucer. Place an egg cup over the yolk to cover it completely and hold it firmly in place, then tip the saucer and pour the egg white into a small bowl.

3. Roll out dough on a lightly floured surface to a 14-inch (35 cm) circle. Carefully roll pastry around rolling pin; unroll pastry onto prepared pizza pan. (Pastry will hang over edge of pan.)

4. **Filling:** In a large bowl, stir together blackberries, peaches, sugar, flour, lemon zest, cinnamon, nutmeg and salt. Spoon mixture onto center of pastry circle, leaving a 3-inch (7.5 cm) border around the edge. Fold pastry border over fruit, pinching pastry to form rough pleats (fruit will not be completely covered). Brush pastry with reserved egg white (from Step 1); sprinkle with granulated sugar.

5. Bake for 40 to 45 minutes or until pastry is golden and fruit is bubbly. Let pie cool on pizza pan to room temperature. Cut into wedges; divide among individual dessert plates. Serve garnished with whipped cream and sprigs of fresh mint.

> ### Make Ahead
> Pastry can be refrigerated, tightly wrapped, for up to 3 days; let stand at room temperature for 30 minutes before rolling out.

Rhubarb-strawberry cobbler with candied ginger

Serves 6

You can omit the ginger from this old-fashioned dessert if you prefer, but it goes beautifully with the rhubarb and adds a flavor boost to the crème fraîche.

Kitchen Wisdom

In its native France, crème fraîche was traditionally made by letting unpasteurized cream stand until it developed a slightly sour flavor. My method of making it is quicker — and safer — and the slightly tart flavor goes well with all kinds of desserts. Try crème fraîche, leaving out the ginger syrup, with other desserts such as Chocolate-Almond Cake (see recipe, page 174) or Exotic Fruit Salad (see recipe, page 152).

- 8-inch (2 L) square baking dish

Fruit Layer

4 cups	sliced fresh rhubarb (about 1 lb/ 500 g) or frozen rhubarb, partially thawed and patted dry	1 L
2 cups	hulled sliced strawberries	500 mL
1/4 cup	granulated sugar	50 mL
1/4 cup	finely chopped candied ginger in syrup, drained (reserve syrup for crème fraîche)	50 mL
1 tbsp	all-purpose flour	15 mL

Topping

1 cup	all-purpose flour	250 mL
3 tbsp	granulated sugar	45 mL
2 tsp	baking powder	10 mL
Pinch	salt	Pinch
1/4 cup	cold butter, cut into pieces	50 mL
3/4 cup	sour cream	175 mL

Ginger Crème Fraîche

1/3 cup	whipping (35%) cream	75 mL
2/3 cup	sour cream	150 mL
2 tbsp	ginger syrup (reserved from candied ginger)	25 mL

1. **Fruit Layer:** Preheat oven to 375°F (190°C). In baking dish, stir together rhubarb, strawberries, sugar, ginger and flour. Set aside.

2. **Topping:** In a food processor, combine flour, 2 tbsp (25 mL) sugar, baking powder and salt; process until combined. Add butter; process until mixture resembles fine crumbs. Add sour cream; process until a soft sticky dough forms.

Kitchen Wisdom

Look for candied ginger in the jams and jellies section of your supermarket or in your local bulk food store. Try it finely chopped over fresh cantaloupe or stirred into a fruit salad.

3. Drop dough in 6 spoonfuls evenly over fruit in baking dish. (Fruit will not be completely covered.) Sprinkle evenly with remaining sugar. Bake for 35 to 40 minutes or until topping has risen and is golden brown, and fruit is bubbly. Serve warm with Ginger Crème Fraîche.

4. **Ginger Crème Fraîche:** Place a medium bowl and the beaters of electric mixer in the freezer; chill for 15 minutes. Pour whipping cream into chilled bowl; beat with electric mixer at high speed until soft peaks just start to form (cream should still be slightly runny). With a large spoon or rubber spatula and using a gentle, cutting motion, fold in sour cream and ginger syrup until well combined. Refrigerate until ready to serve.

Viennese chocolate triangle cake

Serves 6

On a trip to the Austrian capital of Vienna a few years ago, I happily munched my way around the city's famous coffee houses, sampling pastries here, chocolate cakes there — all in the name of research! I tried this cake created by Chef Roman Schida, at Vienna's lavish Hotel Imperial. My version is a little easier to make (since it uses a frozen pound cake), but it's just as decadent and is certain to impress. Don't be put off by the lengthy instructions; if you follow them carefully and refer to the diagram (see below) and photograph (across from page 161), the cake is really quite simple to prepare.

Butter Cream

2 tbsp	boiling water	25 mL
2 tbsp	unsweetened cocoa powder	25 mL
½ cup	unsalted butter, softened	125 mL
2 cups	icing sugar, sifted	500 mL
1 tbsp	milk	15 mL

Cake

1	frozen loaf-shaped pound cake, about 10 oz (300 g)	1
8 oz	good-quality semi-sweet chocolate, coarsely chopped	250 g
¼ cup	unsalted butter	50 mL
1 tbsp	vegetable oil	15 mL
	Candied violets, edible flowers or gold leaf (available from cake decorating stores)	

1. **Butter Cream:** In a small bowl, combine water and cocoa; stir until smooth. Set aside. In a medium bowl, beat butter until creamy. Beat in 1 cup (250 mL) icing sugar until light and fluffy. Add cocoa mixture, milk and remaining icing sugar; beat until smooth and fluffy. (Don't worry if butter cream curdles slightly.) Cover; set aside.

2. **Cake:** Unwrap pound cake; place on a sheet of wax paper (to prevent cake from sticking) on work surface. With a long sharp knife, trim rounded top from cake to form a flat surface. With cake sitting flat on work surface, cut in half horizontally. With each half sitting flat on work surface, carefully cut each horizontally into 3 thin slices.

3. Set aside the slice from bottom of cake. Spread each of the remaining 5 slices of cake with about 2 tbsp (25 mL) butter cream; stack slices neatly on top of each other. Transfer cake to a platter. Measure out ⅔ cup (150 mL) butter cream and set aside; spread remaining butter cream evenly over sides of cake. (The cake should be completely covered with butter cream.) Freeze for 1 hour or until firm.

Edible flowers — such as lavender, bergamot, pansies, forget-me-nots, impatiens or geraniums — make a stunning garnish for many desserts. Use flowers from your own garden, making sure they're free of chemical sprays, or from an organic grower. Remember that not all flowers are edible, so if you're unsure about any, don't use them.

4. Remove cake from freezer. Stand frozen cake vertically on 1 short end. With a long sharp knife, make a diagonal cut crosswise through 1 short end to the opposite short end to form 2 long wedges (see diagram).

5. Place reserved cake slice on a wire rack standing over a sheet of wax paper. Spread with 2 tbsp (25 mL) reserved butter cream. Arrange the 2 wedges of cake, with long frosted sides meeting, on top of the reserved slice to make a long triangle shape. Spread remaining butter cream over the cake to cover it completely, filling any cracks. Freeze for 30 minutes.

6. Meanwhile, in the top half of a double boiler or in a heatproof bowl standing over a saucepan of hot (not boiling) water, melt chocolate with butter and vegetable oil, stirring occasionally until smooth. (Alternatively, microwave on Medium for 2 minutes or until smooth, stirring once.) Let cool to room temperature. Spoon chocolate over cake to cover it completely, using a spatula to smooth the surface. Let cake stand on wire rack until the excess chocolate has dripped onto wax paper and chocolate has firmed up slightly.

7. Using 2 spatulas, carefully transfer cake to a serving platter. Refrigerate for at least 8 hours or up to 24 hours before serving. Garnish with candied violets, edible flowers or flecks of gold leaf.

Make Ahead
Cake must be refrigerated for at least 8 hours or up to 24 hours. It also freezes well.

Roasted pears with ginger cream

Serves 6

Ginger adds mellow flavor to this comforting — and quickly made — winter dessert.

Kitchen Wisdom

Look for candied ginger in the jams and jellies section of your supermarket or in your local bulk food store. Try it finely chopped over fresh cantaloupe or stirred into a fruit salad.

To make skillet handle ovenproof, cover with a double layer of foil.

- Heavy ovenproof skillet large enough to hold pear halves in a single layer

¼ cup	fresh lemon juice	50 mL
6	ripe pears	6
1 tbsp	butter	15 mL
⅓ cup	finely chopped candied ginger in syrup, drained (reserve syrup)	75 mL
1½ cups	whipping (35%) cream	375 mL
3 tbsp	ginger syrup (reserved from ginger)	45 mL
	Fresh mint sprigs	

1. Preheat oven to 400°F (200°C). Pour lemon juice into a medium bowl. With a vegetable peeler or sharp knife, peel pears by paring the skin lengthwise from stem end to wide end of each. Cut pears in half and, using a melon baller or small teaspoon, remove core from each half. With a sharp knife, cut out any woody stem area. As each pear half is prepared, immediately add it to lemon juice, tossing gently to coat.

2. In the skillet, melt butter over medium-high heat. Using a slotted spoon, remove pears from lemon juice. Place them cut-side down in skillet; discard lemon juice. Cook, uncovered, for 2 to 3 minutes or until pears are lightly browned. Remove skillet from heat; turn pears over. Divide ginger evenly among cavities in pears. Transfer skillet to oven; roast pears, uncovered, for 10 to 20 minutes or until very tender.

3. Wearing oven mitts, remove skillet from oven. Remove pears from skillet to a warm plate; keep warm. Whisk cream and ginger syrup into cooking juices remaining in the skillet. Bring to a boil over high heat, scraping up any brown bits from bottom of skillet. Divide pears among 6 dessert plates; drizzle evenly with ginger cream. Garnish each with a mint sprig; serve at once.

Chocolate–Grand Marnier fondue

Serves 4 to 6

This decadent fondue, which will endear you to all the chocoholics in your life, should only be served after the lightest of main courses. Use the best-quality eating, not baking, chocolate you can find for this recipe.

Kitchen Wisdom

A miniature bottle of Grand Marnier (airline size) contains the ¼ cup (50 mL) needed for this recipe.

• Fondue pot and fondue forks

6 oz	good-quality bittersweet chocolate, coarsely chopped	175 g
6 oz	good-quality semi-sweet chocolate, coarsely chopped	175 g
¾ cup	half-and-half (10%) cream	175 mL
¼ cup	Grand Marnier	50 mL
1 tsp	finely grated orange zest	5 mL

Accompaniments

Cubed pound cake, ladyfingers; fresh strawberries or cherries, seedless grapes, dried apricots, orange segments; cubed or sliced banana, apple or pear (tossed in lemon juice); cubed pineapple, peach, mango or kiwi

1. In the top half of a double boiler or in a heatproof bowl standing over a saucepan of hot (not boiling) water, melt bittersweet and semi-sweet chocolate with cream, stirring occasionally until smooth. Remove from heat; stir in Grand Marnier and orange zest.

2. Meanwhile, arrange your chosen accompaniments attractively on a large serving platter, along with fondue forks.

3. Pour chocolate mixture into fondue pot set over a fondue burner. Light burner. Serve with accompaniments for dipping.

Creamy lemon tart

Serves 6 to 8

The filling for this simple ultra-lemony tart magically thickens when you add the lemon juice to the other ingredients. Be sure to use sweetened condensed milk (which is thick and sticky), rather than evaporated milk or the recipe just won't work. If you prefer, serve the tart with Raspberry Sauce (see recipe, page 162), instead of fresh fruit.

Kitchen Wisdom

Store lemons in the fridge and, before using, wash them in warm soapy water, then rinse and dry well. This removes any waxy coating from the lemons, allowing the flavorful oils to be released when you grate the zest. To squeeze as much juice as possible from the fruit, roll them on the counter with the palm of your hand before cutting them in half.

A citrus zester is one of my favorite gadgets, so much so that I have at least two knocking around in my kitchen. Small-handled utensils that have an odd-looking blade with tiny holes in it, zesters are invaluable for scraping every last vestige of colored zest from citrus fruit.

• 9-inch (2.5 L) springform pan, buttered

Half	package (8 oz/250 g) vanilla wafers (about 38 wafers)	Half
2 tbsp	butter	25 mL
3	lemons	3
1	can (10.5 oz/300 mL) sweetened condensed milk	1
¾ cup	sour cream	175 mL
	Fresh raspberries, blueberries or sliced strawberries	

1. Preheat oven to 350°F (180°C). In a food processor, process wafers until fine crumbs form. Add butter; process until well combined. Press crumb mixture evenly over bottom and three-quarters of the way up sides of springform pan. Bake for 8 to 10 minutes or until pale golden around the edges. Remove from oven; let cool to room temperature.

2. With a citrus zester or using the fine holes of a cheese grater, grate zest from lemons, avoiding white pith. If using a zester, chop zest finely. Put zest in a medium bowl. Squeeze juice from lemons through a sieve into a small bowl.

3. Add condensed milk and sour cream to lemon zest; whisk until smooth. Gradually whisk in lemon juice, continuing to whisk until mixture thickens. Pour lemon filling into crust. Refrigerate for at least 4 hours or cover loosely with plastic wrap and refrigerate for up to 12 hours.

4. To serve, run a knife around sides of tart; release sides of pan. Slide tart onto a serving plate. Garnish with raspberries, blueberries or sliced strawberries around edge of tart. Cut into wedges with a damp knife.

Make Ahead
The tart must be refrigerated for at least 4 hours, but can be refrigerated, covered, for up to 12 hours.

Kiwi mousse

Kiwi, that quintessential fruit of the 1970s, is finally becoming trendy again. This quick-fix mousse combines the flavors of lime and kiwi in a tropical-tasting dessert.

Kitchen Wisdom

You'll need ripe kiwis for this recipe; they should yield to gentle pressure when you cup them in the palm of your hand.

- 6 individual dessert dishes or large wine glasses

6	ripe kiwi fruit	6
2	limes	2
1/2 cup	granulated sugar	125 mL
1	package (1/4 oz/7 g) unflavored gelatin	1
1 cup	whipping (35%) cream	250 mL

1. Place a medium bowl and the beaters of electric mixer in the freezer; chill for 15 minutes. With a sharp knife, peel kiwi fruit. Cut 6 slices from 1 kiwi; set aside. Chop remaining fruit coarsely.

2. Cut 6 thin slices from 1 lime; set aside. Grate zest from other lime. Squeeze juice from whole lime and uncut half of first lime. In a food processor, combine chopped kiwi, lime zest, lime juice and sugar; process until smooth.

3. Pour 1/4 cup (50 mL) kiwi mixture into a small heatproof bowl. Pour remaining kiwi mixture into a medium bowl. Sprinkle gelatin over kiwi mixture in heatproof bowl; set aside for 10 minutes or until gelatin is puffy.

4. Pour cream into chilled bowl; beat with electric mixer at high speed until the cream holds soft peaks.

5. Set bowl containing kiwi and gelatin mixture in a saucepan of hot water. Stir for 1 minute or until gelatin has dissolved. Stir gelatin mixture into rest of kiwi mixture.

6. With a large spoon or rubber spatula and using a gentle cutting motion, gradually fold kiwi mixture into whipped cream until well combined. Divide kiwi mousse evenly among dishes. Refrigerate, tightly covered, for at least 4 hours or until set. Serve garnished with reserved kiwi and lime slices.

> **Make Ahead**
> The desserts must be chilled for at least 4 hours, but can be refrigerated, tightly covered, for up to 24 hours. Let stand at room temperature for 30 minutes before serving.

Chocolate-almond cake

Serves 6 to 8

This dense fudgey cake is very rich — so serve it in small wedges with dollops of softly whipped cream or a drizzle of Raspberry Sauce (see recipe, page 162) and a handful of fresh berries. Be careful not to overbake the cake; it should still be moist in the center.

Kitchen Wisdom

The easiest way to separate the white and yolk of an egg is to break the egg onto a saucer. Place an egg cup over the yolk to cover it completely and hold it firmly in place, then tip the saucer and pour the egg white into a small bowl.

- 8-inch (2 L) springform pan
- Sheet of wax paper or parchment paper

6 oz	good-quality semi-sweet chocolate, coarsely chopped	175 g
⅓ cup	unsalted butter, softened	75 mL
¼ cup	granulated sugar	50 mL
3	eggs, separated	3
¾ cup	ground almonds	175 mL
1¾ cups	soft bread crumbs	425 mL
	Whipped cream	
	Toasted sliced almonds	

1. Preheat oven to 350°F (180°C). Use springform pan to trace a circle on the wax paper. Cut out circle, cutting slightly within the traced circle. Lightly butter base and sides of pan; put paper circle in base of pan. Set aside.

2. In the top half of a double boiler or in a heatproof bowl standing over a saucepan of hot (not boiling) water, melt chocolate, stirring occasionally until smooth. (Alternatively, microwave on Medium for 2 minutes, stirring once.) Remove chocolate from heat; let cool slightly.

3. In a large bowl, with an electric mixer beat together butter and sugar until light and fluffy. Beat in egg yolks one at a time, beating well after each addition. Beat in chocolate and ground almonds. Stir in bread crumbs.

4. In another bowl, with clean beaters, beat egg whites on high speed until stiff peaks form. With a large spoon or rubber spatula and using a gentle cutting motion, fold egg whites into chocolate mixture until well combined and no white streaks remain.

5. Spoon chocolate mixture into prepared pan, smoothing surface level. Bake for 30 to 35 minutes or until center of cake springs back when touched lightly. (Do not overbake; cake should still be moist in the center.)

6. Run a knife around inside edge of pan; let cake cool completely in pan on a wire rack. Release sides of pan; slide cake onto a serving platter, removing paper. Serve garnished with whipped cream and toasted sliced almonds.

Variation

Cut cake into wedges and place each wedge on an individual dessert plate. Top each wedge with a drained, halved poached pear (see recipe, page 158), drizzle with Mum's Chocolate Sauce (see recipe, page 184) and top each with a dollop of softly whipped cream.

Make Ahead
Cake can be baked up to 24 hours ahead; wrap then store at room temperature.

Spiced rhubarb tart

Serves 6

This easy pie is a lovely springtime treat when the first stalks of local rhubarb appear in the stores.

Kitchen Wisdom

If fresh rhubarb is unavailable, substitute frozen; there's no need to thaw it.

Make Ahead

Tart can be refrigerated, covered, for up to 24 hours; let stand at room temperature for 30 minutes before serving.

• Baking sheet

1	frozen 9-inch (22.5 cm) pie shell	1
2 cups	sliced rhubarb (about 8 oz/ 250 g) or partially thawed frozen rhubarb, patted dry	500 mL
1	can (5 oz/160 mL) evaporated milk	1
1/3 cup	packed brown sugar	75 mL
1	egg	1
3 tbsp	all-purpose flour	45 mL
1/4 tsp	ground cinnamon	1 mL
1/4 tsp	ground ginger	1 mL
	Vanilla ice cream or softly whipped cream	

1. Preheat oven to 400°F (200°C). Put pie shell on baking sheet. Line pie shell with foil and weight it with uncooked dried beans. Bake for 8 to 10 minutes. Remove from oven; set aside to cool. Increase oven temperature to 425°F (220°C).

2. Place rhubarb in pie shell, spreading evenly. In a small bowl, whisk together milk, sugar, egg, flour, cinnamon and ginger until mixture is smooth. Pour milk mixture evenly into pie shell.

3. Bake for 30 minutes or until rhubarb is tender and tart is golden brown. (If pastry browns too much, shield edges of tart with strips of foil.) Serve warm with vanilla ice cream or let cool completely and serve with softly whipped cream.

Caledonian cream with raspberries

Serves 6

My original copy of this recipe is written on yellowed paper, dog-eared and spattered with unidentifiable food stains. I don't even recognize my own handwriting of 25 years ago, but it's a recipe that has stood the test of time. I think I originally copied it from Liz Paterson, one of my oldest, dearest friends — and goodness knows where she got it from.

Kitchen Wisdom

No need to worry if you don't have fancy glass dishes for desserts like this. Wine glasses, small china ramekins or custard cups — even fancy tea cups — work just as well. I've even spooned the Caledonian Cream into cut-glass scotch tumblers, much to my Scottish husband's chagrin.

When raspberries aren't in season, substitute fresh sliced strawberries or blueberries.

A miniature bottle of Drambuie or scotch whisky (airline size) contains the ¼ cup (50 mL) needed for this recipe.

• 6 individual glass dishes or large wine glasses

¾ cup	orange marmalade	175 mL
¼ cup	Drambuie or scotch whisky	50 mL
2 tbsp	granulated sugar	25 mL
1½ cups	whipping (35%) cream	375 mL
2 cups	fresh raspberries	500 mL
6	sprigs fresh mint	6

1. Put a large bowl and the beaters of electric mixer in the freezer; chill for 15 minutes.

2. In a small bowl, whisk together marmalade, Drambuie and sugar until most of the sugar has dissolved.

3. Pour cream into chilled bowl; beat with electric mixer on high speed just until it starts to thicken. Gradually beat in marmalade mixture, continuing to beat until soft peaks form.

4. Reserving 12 of the best-looking raspberries for garnish, divide remaining raspberries evenly among dishes. Spoon cream mixture over raspberries, dividing evenly. Serve garnished with reserved raspberries and mint sprigs.

> ### Make Ahead
> The desserts, without garnish, can be refrigerated, tightly covered, for up to 8 hours; let stand at room temperature for 30 minutes before serving.

Figs poached in mulled wine with spiced cream

Serves 6

This is my version of a heavenly dessert I enjoyed at The Pheasant, a splendid pub in the village of Keyston in southern England. The Pheasant looked as if it came straight out of a Miss Marple movie: thatched roof, hollyhocks framing the windows outside, and the locals quietly sipping pints at the bar. The pub's chef, Martin Lee, combined red wine, spices and dried fruit in this dessert; it tastes to me like the whole of Christmas in a bowl.

- Large nonreactive skillet

2	3-inch (7.5 cm) cinnamon sticks	2
1 cup	whipping (35%) cream	250 mL
8	whole cloves	8
3 cups	full-bodied red wine, such as Cabernet Sauvignon	750 mL
½ cup	granulated sugar	125 mL
24	dried Calimyrna figs (about 1 lb/500 g), stems removed	24
1	orange, thinly sliced	1
	Ground cinnamon	

1. Break 1 cinnamon stick into pieces. In a small saucepan over medium heat, stir together broken cinnamon stick, cream and 4 cloves. Heat for 2 minutes or just until small bubbles start to form around the edge. Remove from heat; let cool to room temperature. Refrigerate until chilled.

2. Meanwhile, in the skillet, stir together wine, sugar, remaining cinnamon stick and cloves. Add figs and orange slices; bring to a boil over high heat, stirring occasionally to dissolve sugar. Reduce heat to low; simmer, covered, for 1½ hours or until figs are tender but still firm.

3. With a slotted spoon, remove figs to a shallow dish. Discard orange slices. Increase heat to high; bring wine mixture to a boil. Boil for 5 to 7 minutes or until wine mixture is reduced to about ¾ cup (175 mL) and is slightly syrupy. Strain wine mixture through a sieve over figs; stir gently to coat figs with wine mixture. Let cool to room temperature.

Be sure to use Calimyrna figs for this recipe. They're bigger, plumper and have a better texture than the smaller black mission figs. If your supermarket doesn't stock them, try your local bulk food store.

4. Put a medium bowl and the beaters of electric mixer in the freezer; chill for 15 minutes. Strain cream through a fine sieve into chilled bowl. Beat cream on high speed until it holds soft peaks.

5. To serve, divide figs among 6 individual shallow dishes or dessert glasses. Spoon some wine mixture over each portion. Spoon a dollop of spiced cream alongside or on top of figs. Sprinkle cream with a little cinnamon, serve at once.

Variation

Packed in small sterilized jars, the figs make great hostess or Christmas gifts — just remember to keep them refrigerated.

Make Ahead
Poached figs and spiced cream can be refrigerated, covered and in separate dishes, for up to 24 hours.

CHEAT'S DESSERTS

The following recipes are my secret weapons. They're all easy — almost instant — desserts that will knock the socks off the most jaded dinner guests. There's only one golden rule to remember: use the best-quality ingredients you can find for these short cuts. For example, top-grade ice cream can cost a little more but think of the time and effort you're saving — and of the accolades that will come your way.

Fruit sherbet Fitzgerald

Serves 6

I enjoyed this ridiculously easy dessert on a rooftop in Córdoba in southern Spain with a group of good friends, among them my buddy and reluctant food writer John Fitzgerald, who took great delight in thinking up names — most of them unprintable — for the combination of fruit sherbet and sparkling wine.

Prepare it immediately before serving and for best — and frothiest — results, make sure you use fruit sherbet rather than sorbet. Any fruit sherbet can be used but orange, lemon or lime are the most refreshing.

Kitchen Wisdom

There's no need to buy expensive French Champagne for this dessert; look for dry Spanish *cava*, which is just as good and often a third of the price.

• Six tall glasses

4 cups	fruit sherbet	1 L
3 cups	dry sparkling wine (such as Spanish *cava*), chilled	750 mL
6	sprigs fresh mint	6
6	thin strips lemon zest	6

1. Divide sherbet evenly among the glasses. Pour wine over sherbet, dividing evenly.

2. Garnish each glass with a mint sprig and a strip of lemon zest. Serve at once.

Honey-orange yogurt with fresh fruit

Serves 6

Mediterranean-style desserts like this one couldn't be simpler or more delicious. Prepare a colorful platter of fresh fruit — such as sliced melon and peaches (tossed in lemon juice), orange segments, halved fresh figs or whole strawberries — and serve it with this delicately flavored yogurt to spoon over each serving.

Kitchen Wisdom

You need only half an orange to flavor the yogurt, so peel and segment the other half and add it to the fruit platter.

2 cups	Balkan-style plain yogurt	500 mL
2 tbsp	liquid honey	25 mL
Half	small orange	Half
	Fresh fruit	

1. In a medium serving bowl, stir together yogurt and honey. Grate zest and squeeze juice from orange half. Add zest and juice to yogurt; stir until well combined. Serve with fresh fruit.

Make Ahead
Yogurt mixture can be refrigerated, covered, for up to 24 hours.

Baked apples on cinnamon-raisin toast

Serves 6

If you give this super-fast recipe its traditional French name, pommes en croûte, *none of your guests will guess how easy it is to make. Serve hot with scoops of good-quality vanilla ice cream.*

Kitchen Wisdom

Don't use Northern Spy apples for this recipe; they're too firm.

- Baking sheet

1/3 cup	butter, melted	75 mL
6	1/2-inch (1 cm) thick slices cinnamon-raisin bread	6
2 tbsp	granulated sugar	25 mL
3	McIntosh or Empire apples, peeled, cored and thinly sliced	3
1 tbsp	fresh lemon juice	15 mL
1/2 tsp	ground cinnamon (optional)	2 mL

1. Preheat oven to 400°F (200°C). Pour butter into a wide shallow dish. Quickly dip one side of each bread slice into butter. Arrange in a single layer, butter-side down, on baking sheet. Sprinkle evenly with half the sugar.

2. Arrange apple slices in overlapping rows over bread, covering slices completely. Brush with remaining butter. Sprinkle with lemon juice, cinnamon and remaining sugar. Bake for 20 minutes or until apple slices are tender and starting to brown. Divide among individual plates; serve at once.

Sam's butterscotch sauce

Makes about 2 cups (500 mL)

Drizzle this almost-instant sauce over good-quality ice cream, add fresh berries and/or a crisp cookie and you have an impressive dessert in minutes. Equally delicious (and just as quick) is Mum's Chocolate Sauce (see recipe, next page).

My good friend Julie Cohen handed out little beribboned jars of this delectable sauce at the baby shower to herald the arrival of her son Sam — a sweet treat to celebrate a sweet boy. Serve with vanilla, butter-pecan, chocolate or white chocolate chip ice cream.

Kitchen Wisdom

For an easy, mess-free way to measure corn syrup or other sticky ingredients, spray a liquid measure with baking spray before pouring in the syrup.

For a grown-up version of this sauce, stir in 2 tbsp (25 mL) brandy or rum before serving.

1¼ cups	packed brown sugar	300 mL
⅔ cup	corn syrup	150 mL
¼ cup	butter	50 mL
Pinch	salt	Pinch
1	can (5 oz/160 mL) evaporated milk	1

1. In a saucepan over medium heat, combine brown sugar, corn syrup, butter and salt; cook, stirring often, for 2 minutes or until butter and sugar have melted.

2. Increase heat to medium-high; boil for 1 to 2 minutes or until temperature registers 234°F (112°C) on a candy thermometer or a little of the mixture dropped into a small bowl of cold water forms a soft ball.

3. Remove saucepan from heat; let cool for 5 minutes. Whisk in milk until mixture is smooth. Serve at once or let cool completely.

Make Ahead

Sauce can be refrigerated in a sealed jar for up to 1 month. Serve cold, or reheat in a double boiler (or in a heatproof bowl over a saucepan of hot [not boiling] water), until bubbly. Or microwave on High for 1 to 2 minutes, stirring once.

Mum's chocolate sauce

Makes about 1 cup (250 mL)

This was a favorite standby of my mother's when we were kids and was frequently requested at family birthday parties. The sauce sets into a toffee-like coating as soon as it hits the cold ice cream. Serve with vanilla, banana, orange, coffee or chocolate ice cream. Don't be tempted to add all the ingredients to the saucepan at once — it just won't work.

• Small nonstick saucepan

½ cup	butter	125 mL
½ cup	corn syrup	125 mL
¼ cup	unsweetened cocoa powder	50 mL

1. In saucepan over medium heat, combine butter and corn syrup; cook, stirring occasionally, for 2 to 3 minutes or until butter has melted.

2. Remove saucepan from heat; whisk in cocoa until no lumps remain. Return saucepan to medium heat; simmer, whisking often, for 2 minutes or until sauce is bubbly and shiny. Serve at once.

Make Ahead
Sauce can be refrigerated, covered, for up to 3 days. Reheat over medium-low heat, stirring often, until bubbly and hot, or microwave on High for 1 to 2 minutes, stirring once.

Library and Archives Canada Cataloguing in Publication

Aitken, Julia
   125 best entertaining recipes / Julia Aitken.

Includes index.
Previously published under title: Julia Aitken's easy entertaining cookbook.
ISBN 978-0-7788-0161-0

1. Cookery. 2. Entertaining. I. Aitken, Julia, 1955–. Julia Aitken's easy entertaining cookbook.
II. Title. III. Title: One hundred twenty-five best entertaining recipes.

TX731.A37 2007   642'.4   C2007-903026-2

Index

Spanish-style:
  green beans, 127
  mushroom appetizers, 17
Spiced pear biscuits, 65
Spinach and watercress salad, 138
Squash with farfalle and garlic cream, 50–51
Stew:
  beef, 96
  vegetable, 134–35
Stir-fry, snow pea and mushroom, 133
Stock, giblet, 84–85, 92–93
Strawberry ice cream, 149
Strawberry-rhubarb cobbler, 166–67
Streusel, 161
Stuffing, apple-thyme, 94
Sun-dried tomatoes:
  to chop, 144
  potato temptation, 122
Swordfish, with tomatoes and feta, 69

T

Tandoori chicken with mango dip, 20–21
Tapenade, crusted lamb racks, 116
Tarte tatin, onion, 82
Tarts:
  lemon, 172
  rhubarb, 176
  tomato and blue cheese, 29
  watercress and feta, 78–79
  See also Pastry; Pie
Tex-Mex marinade, 100–101
Thai-style:
  chicken and coconut soup, 40
  fish parcels, 70
  roasted shrimp, 14

Tomato(es):
  and arugula with ricotta, 26
  beef curry, 97
  and blue cheese tart, 29
  -fennel focaccia, 53
  pizza, 62
  salad, 144
  See also Sun-dried tomatoes
Tuna, with tomatoes and feta, 69
Turkey roast, 92–93
Turmeric, about, 44

V

Vegetables:
  with roasted-garlic couscous, 76–77
  shrimp and pasta with, 60–61
  stew, 134–35
Viennese chocolate triangle cake, 168–69
Vinaigrette:
  lemon-dill, 143
  sherry, 142
  See also Dressing

W

Walnuts, mushroom and prosciutto antipasto, 33
Watercress:
  and feta tart, 78–79
  and spinach salad, 138
Watermelon, and cherry tomato brochettes, 16
White bean salad with vinaigrette, 143

Y

Yogurt, with fresh fruit, 181